Creating with the Cosmos:

An Astrological Guide to Awakening and Enhancing Creative Power

Emily Trinkaus

Creating With the Cosmos: An Astrological Guide to
Awakening and Enhancing Creative Power

by Emily Trinkaus

Special thanks to Stephanie Shea and Kismet Design Group for
cover design, Mari Saint-Pierre for editing, and Loren McCrory
for helping to birth it into form.

VirgoMagic Press
Portland, Oregon
2012

CONTENTS

Introduction

Creativity for Everyone

"We are all meant to shine, as children do. We were born to make manifest the glory of God that is within us. It's not just in some of us; it's in everyone."

— Marianne Williamson

Remember when you were a kid, getting lost in a game of make-believe, telling fantastic stories, showing off your latest finger painting or macaroni sculpture? For many of us, the natural creativity we expressed as children was dampened or even destroyed by the time we reached adulthood. Pablo Picasso said, "All children are artists. The problem is how to remain an artist once he grows up."

The premise of this book is that you don't need to "learn to be creative" as much as uncover, recover and strengthen your natural, instinctual creator self.

Astrology can be a powerful ally in this process. Part I of this book explores four planets in your birth chart, offering insight into your innate strengths and talents, as well as guidance for activating and sustaining your creative life. Part II shows you simple, practical ways to work with the planetary cycles for greater ease and success in your creative ventures.

Creativity is not just about artistic expression. Creativity is power -- the power to create your life and the world you live in, and to realize your full potential.

As we transition from the Age of Pisces to the Age of Aquarius, we are confronted with unprecedented global crises designed to wake us up out of the illusion of powerlessness. Rather than looking outside ourselves for someone or something to save us, we awaken to our own divine powers, and become the creator gods we've been waiting for.

These critical times require the shining forth of each person's essential and unique creative brilliance. My intention is that this book will support you in awakening and amplifying your creative power, and inspire in you the courage to share your gifts.

Part I

Your Unique Creative Blueprint

An Astrological Cookbook

*"We are born at a given moment, in a given place and,
like vintage years of wine, we have the qualities
of the year and of the season in which we
are born. Astrology does not lay
claim to anything more."*

- CARL JUNG

Your astrological birth chart -- a map of the sky at your exact moment and place of birth -- provides a blueprint of your creative potential. What you do with this potential is up to you. Astrology does not determine your future, but rather points to your innate talents, strengths and possible pitfalls. With this awareness, you increase your chances for success and fulfillment.

If you don't have a copy of your birth chart, you can go to astro. com to get one for free. Once you've identified the sign of your Sun, Moon, Venus and Mars, you're ready to consult the information below. Please note -- because the Moon moves quickly, changing signs every two-and-a-quarter days, knowing your time of birth may be necessary to accurately identify your Moon sign.

The twelve signs of the zodiac roughly correlate with the twelve houses of the birth chart. For example, the Sun in the First House expresses similar qualities to the Sun in Aries, the first sign, while Venus in the Third House is comparable to Venus in Gemini, the third sign. If you have your time of birth, you can identify which house each planet occupies in your chart, and read about that placement for more insight.

Working with the information provided about the Moon, Venus, the Sun and Mars is a powerful starting point for increasing awareness around your creative path and potential. But in truth, all the planets play a role in creative expression. Additionally, the relationships between the planets in your chart -- the aspects they make to one another -- are also a factor.

If you're looking for a more thorough understanding of your creative potential and how to manifest it, I recommend a full reading of your birth chart by a professional astrologer. Some of the suggestions offered here may resonate more strongly for you than others. Please trust your own intuition in following the guidance that feels like a "yes."

Feminine Creativity

The Moon and Venus

"Yet it is in our idleness, our dreams, that the submerged truth sometimes comes to the top."

- VIRGINIA WOOLF

We often think of creativity as making something happen -- asserting the will to manifest a desired outcome. While this masculine or outward aspect of creativity is an essential part of the process, would-be artists can become blocked when they start here. ("I keep pushing and pushing, but nothing is happening!")

Instead, it can be helpful to start with a feminine, more receptive approach to creativity -- setting an appropriate space for the process, acknowledging potential fears and blocks, identifying sources of inspiration and support, and taking time for deep inner listening. Astrologically, this feminine aspect of creativity is represented by the planetary goddesses -- the Moon and Venus.

Ideally, a healthy and sustainable creative life involves a balance between the feminine and masculine -- yin and yang. Understanding and honoring the Moon and Venus aspects of your psyche can help you cultivate the yin side of creativity.

☽

The Moon

Nurturing Your Inner Artist

"Everything is gestation, then bringing forth."
- RAINER MARIA RILKE

The Moon represents the maternal feminine, the wise goddess who gave birth to us all. Just as a pregnant mother-to-be needs a safe and protected space for giving birth, you need to feel secure in order to let your creative brilliance shine.

Your Moon sign reveals the kind of space your inner artist needs to feel safe. Additionally, it shows how to nurture and sustain your creative life, and how to access and enhance your intuition and inspiration.

☽ ♈

Moon in Aries
or in the 1st House

*"To grow in craft is to increase the breadth of what
I can do, but art is the depth, the passion, the desire,
the courage to be myself and myself alone."*
                                        - PAT SCHNEIDER

As the first sign of the Zodiac, Aries is the trailblazer, the innovator and the warrior. With your Moon in the sign of the Ram, you need a creative space where you can feel free and independent, and where you get to be in charge. Your fiery spirit likes to be surrounded by reds, oranges, yellows and golds. You might need to make frequent changes in your space to satisfy your need for novelty.

Creative expression provides a much-needed outlet for your passionate, emotional nature. Feelings of impatience, irritation and frustration may be cries for attention from your inner artist. Let anger build into outrage, and channel that powerful energy into inspired works of art. The more you express your fiery feelings through your art, the more you fuel your creative passion.

If you're feeling creatively blocked, it might be time to experiment with a new form of expression. If you're a painter, join a writing group; if you're a pianist, take a cooking class. Trying something new brings you back to "beginner's mind," allowing you to see the world with innocent eyes and a fresh perspective. In this state, you feel re-inspired to create.

Physical exercise is essential to feeling balanced, reducing stress and anxiety, and sustaining a long-term creative life. You've got a lot of energy to burn, and without regular exercise you might feel too wound-up to concentrate on creativity. Martial arts, yoga and Pilates are especially recommended, to cultivate the self-discipline and strength that feed your warrior spirit.

While you do need to take on heroic challenges, beware of going overboard and taking on so much that you burn out. Asking for help when you need it is a sign of strength, and learning to delegate frees up time for your creative pursuits. When you honestly express your thoughts and feelings, you receive the support you need to move forward.

☽ ♉
Moon in Taurus
or in the 2nd House

"I feel that art has something to do with the achievement of stillness in the midst of chaos. A stillness which characterizes prayer, too, and the eye of the storm. I think that art has something to do with an arrest of attention in the midst of distraction."

- SAUL BELLOW

The Moon finds her highest expression in the sign of the Bull, according to traditional astrology. Here is the Great Mother at her most abundant, sensual and fertile. You possess an overflowing supply of creative energy, sourced in your deep connection with the Earth.

Your creative space best serves you when all your senses are delighted and you are surrounded by nature. Even in a small apartment in the city, you can fill your space with house plants, fresh flowers, stones, crystals, feathers and other reminders of Mother Earth. You have a special talent for creating beautiful spaces, and you tend to work best when you feel rooted in a stable and comfortable home base.

No matter how rowdy other aspects of your personality may be, you require periodic bouts of stillness and silence, time for simply being, when you can access your deepest creative imagination. Music (both playing and listening) can be a significant resource for journeying into the depths. You have an affinity with drumming and other ways of keeping the beat, and with singing (Taurus rules the throat).

Take excellent care of your creative spirit by nurturing your body with healthy self-care routines. Since Taurus can have a tendency toward laziness, exercise might be the arena where your self-care falls short. Establishing a daily habit of walking and stretching, even for just fifteen minutes a day, can make all the difference in how you feel.

While you do need your routines and rituals, when you get overly attached to certain ways of being or thinking, you become rigid and lose your creative juiciness. Letting go of what has become stagnant makes room for an infusion of fresh, invigorating energy. You might have a tendency to go overboard in the nesting department, so make sure to leave your house from time to time and break your routine.

When you nurture Mother Earth, through environmentally conscious actions or simply through your gratitude for all She provides, you are rewarded with increased creative energy.

☽ ♊

Moon in Gemini
or in the 3rd House

*"A writer lives, at best, in a state of astonishment.
Beneath any feeling he has of the good or evil of the
world lies a deeper one of wonder at it all."*

- WILLIAM SANSOM

With the Moon in the sign of the Twins, you need a creative space that reflects your playful and inquisitive nature, and your need for variety. You might feel compelled to move the furniture around every so often, just to keep things interesting. To occupy and enchant your busy mind -- an absolute necessity for personal happiness -- it's helpful to surround yourself with books, magazines, and media in many forms.

Adaptable by nature, you could happily create in a variety of spaces, but feel most secure when you have the feeling of openness and freedom -- lots of light, high ceilings, and bright colors (especially yellow and chartreuse). Feathers, mobiles, wind chimes, climbing plants, and images of birds and butterflies all help you connect with Air, your elemental source of inspiration.

Bored by sameness, and a natural multi-tasker, you feel comfortable juggling two or more creative projects at a time. Variety not only adds spice to your life but is essential for sustaining creative inspiration. You have a gift for working in multiple fields and bringing together disparate art forms, though you may have a special affinity for writing and film.

Just like Peter Pan, your mind never has to grow old, as long as you keep alive your curiosity and wonder. Cultivate these parts of yourself by traveling, making connections with people of different ages and backgrounds, and taking classes or workshops in subjects you know nothing about but find interesting. Recording thoughts and observations in a journal (you're a natural reporter) helps you identify connections between experiences, and provides an outlet for your abundant mental energy.

Balance your need for mental and social stimulation by taking time to connect with your inner depths. Music (listening to or playing) is a significant resource, and you have a special affinity with the piano, stringed instruments, the clarinet and flute.

Physical or meditative activities that emphasize the mind/body connection (yoga, Pilates, martial arts) help you feel grounded so you can access your deepest wisdom and intuition. Creative burn-out can signal that you're spending too much time in your brain, and your body needs some attention.

Moon in Cancer
or in the 4th House

"A work of art which did not begin in emotion is not art."
- PAUL CEZANNE

At home in the sign of the Crab, the Moon in watery Cancer is highly sensitive, intuitive, nurturing and resourceful. Your rich imagination and extensive memory bank provide infinite material to sustain your abundant creativity.

Like the Crab in her shell, you need a creative space that feels like a safe retreat from the potentially threatening outside world. You like to feel comfy, cozy and free to get lost in your dreams and fantasies. You are happiest when you can have -- if not an entire room or studio -- at least one corner to call your own (you might actually prefer small spaces). The color silver connects you with the magical Moon, and deep shades of blue with the Water element. Shells, sand and the sound of ocean waves bring you in touch with the source of your power.

With your strong connection to history, and especially ancestors, you feel creatively inspired when surrounded by reminders from the past -- family photos, objects passed down for generations, and souvenirs from joyful times with loved ones. However, you can feel stuck and stagnant if your space is overly cluttered with memorabilia. Use your intuition to discern which possessions truly feed you, and which drain your energy. When you let go of what you no longer need or love, your creative inspiration flows.

Your highly attuned emotional antennae pick up on all the nuances of your environment and give you a wealth of material to channel into creative projects. Your challenge is not to get so overwhelmed by emotions that you feel burnt-out and have no energy for your creativity. Your sensitive stomach (ruled by Cancer) is a good barometer of your emotional state, and will tell you when it's time to get back into your shell to decompress. Physical exercise, especially swimming, dancing and walking, are also helpful for shaking off other people's energy and bringing you back to center.

You can enhance your creativity and intuition by cultivating your relationship with the Moon -- gazing at her, conversing with her, and paying attention to her cycles. Using a lunar calendar you can track the Moon's waxing and waning to get clues to your own creative cycles. As the Moon is waxing (growing) you'll feel a surge of expansive energy; this is the time to start new projects and really go for it. After the Full Moon, as the Moon diminishes, you'll feel your own energy wane. This is the time to complete projects and then turn inward again to relax and recharge your batteries, preparing for the next cycle, which begins with the New Moon.

☽ ♌

Moon in Leo
or in the 5th House

"Thank your readers and the critics who praise you, and then ignore them. Write for the most intelligent, wittiest, wisest audience in the universe: Write to please yourself."

- HARLAN ELLISON

Leo the Lion is king of the jungle, and with the Moon in Leo, your creativity flourishes when you pamper yourself with the royal treatment. You need to feel like the king or queen of your castle, and surround yourself only with what delights you and makes you feel special. You feel inspired in a fun, festive, celebratory environment. What's being celebrated, of course, is you.

Yes, your space needs to be functional, but functional can still look fabulous. Bright colors, especially golds and yellows, incite your fiery spirit, while purple pleases your regal soul. Let your space support your need for a little extravagance -- include velvety textures and romantic touches (Leo is the consummate romantic).

Ruled by the Sun, Leo needs to shine brightly, preferably on stage in front of a large and appreciative audience. Even if other parts of your personality are shy and reclusive, there's a part of you that craves attention and applause. Find a creative outlet to satisfy this need, a place in your life where you feel validated for being special. Start by validating yourself -- identify your talents, appreciate what makes you unique, and cultivate self-love. Pay special attention to your Sun sign for guidance about how to channel your creative fire.

With your inclination toward the dramatic (understatement), you have an affinity with all aspects of theater. An excess of emotional drama in your personal life signals the need for more drama in your creative life. Call on your deep reserves of courage (be lionhearted) and take that acting class, write that screenplay, volunteer as a stage hand for a community theater group, work with kids to put on a play . . .

You can sustain your creativity by taking risks, always following your heart and moving toward what feels like fun. Balance your need to be the center of attention with contributing your abundant creative energy toward supporting your friends and community.

What you generously give to others comes back to you many times over.

☽ ♍

Moon in Virgo
or in the 6th House

"Have no fear of perfection, you'll never reach it."
\- SALVADOR DALI

With the Moon in persnickety Virgo, setting up the right space is essential to a productive creative life. You require simplicity, efficiency and neatness, and appreciate mellow earth tones (olive green, beiges and browns) to calm your worrying mind. The hermit in you needs privacy and periodic retreat time in order to delve deeply into your complex mind and imagination. You may be most productive when you're alone, or at least when you can tune out all distractions from the outside world.

You might feel the need to clean your space thoroughly before you jump into the creative process. Your challenge is to know when you're honoring your inner Virgoan goddess, and when you're procrastinating. Your intuition will tell you whether reorganizing the medicine cabinet is truly necessary before getting down to work, or if a simple desk-straightening will suffice.

Enhance the power of your pre-creativity cleaning routine by transforming it into a ritual. Light a candle, and burn sage, cedar or incense to purify your space on an energetic level. As you clean, imagine you are removing not only dust and clutter, but all obstacles to joyful creative expression. Don't forget to ask for help from your invisible but nevertheless powerful friends -- spirit guides, angels, power animals and fairies. Bringing magic, intention and a higher perspective into daily tasks helps you have more fun and align with the creative flow.

Your need to create order extends beyond space clearing. You have a strong sense of service, wanting to apply your skills and talents to healing and perfecting the world. Your challenge is to find a balance between serving others and taking care of yourself.

If you feel drained by too many commitments, use your fine sense of discrimination to discern what's ready to be released. Your sensitive digestive system -- the part of the body ruled by Virgo -- will let you know when you're out of balance. Trust that, by taking time to nurture your body and serve your spirit, you are ultimately of greater service to the collective.

You may have a tendency to want to control your feelings, which can stifle creative expression. When you accept your emotions, and let yourself really feel them -- rather than overanalyzing or needing to make sense out of them -- you have greater access to your intuition and creativity. Writing in a journal helps you process feelings and deepen your awareness.

Spending time in nature feeds your creativity and recharges your creative batteries, while regular exercise helps you get out of your brain and back into your body.

Moon in Libra
or in the 7th House

*"To be creative means to be in love with life. You can be
creative only if you love life enough that you want
to enhance its beauty, you want to bring a little
more music to it, a little more poetry to it,
a little more dance to it."*

\- OSHO

With the Moon in Libra, being surrounded by beauty and elegance is a pre-requisite for creative expression. Extremely sensitive to your environment, you can feel physically ill in an ugly or messy space. Your creative sanctuary should be clean, organized, harmonious, and peaceful -- a retreat from the chaos and clutter of the outside world. Green, especially jade and emerald tones, connects you with your heart chakra, reminding you to create from a place of love. Ruled by Venus, Libra is the lover.

Arts and culture provide significant sustenance for your creative life. Visiting museums and art galleries, attending concerts and plays, and perusing art books and reading literature are all strategies for inspiring your inner artist. Listening to music also inspires you and helps you feel peaceful. You like feeling connected to the wider culture of creativity, seeing how your individual work fits in with and contributes to the greater whole.

Sociable and relationship-oriented by nature, you work well collaborating and partnering with others. At the same time, because you're so sensitive, you may absorb other people's emotions and then feel burnt-out by too much interaction.

You need periodic alone time to decompress and attend to your own needs. You might need to set firm boundaries with friends and family in order to carve out this time for yourself. By taking the risk of making yourself and your creativity a priority, you may temporarily upset the harmony in your relationships, but the peace that comes from honestly expressing your feelings will create a more genuine harmony in the long run.

Your emotions, like the Scales, constantly seek a state of equilibrium. When you feel out of balance, worry and anxiety take over and your creativity is put on hold until the scales realign. Often, returning to balance involves coming back into your body. The Moon in airy Libra feels comfortable living in mental constructs, and sometimes forgets about the physical world. Deep breathing, walking, taking a bath, and stretching are all simple ways to regain inner harmony. From this place of inner peace, you can much more easily create balance and order in your external circumstances.

You might tend to think through your emotions instead of

actually feeling them, and may judge yourself for feelings that seem unkind, unwarranted or illogical. Instead of thinking about how you should, in an ideal universe, feel about a certain situation, risk experiencing your feelings directly, acknowledging and accepting what's true for you right now.

You can increase your creative power and intuition by dropping into the present moment and expressing the full range of your emotional palette. Let your art provide an outlet for expressing these messy feelings without the fear of harming or offending another.

Moon in Scorpio
or in the 8th House

"Creativity -- like human life itself -- begins in darkness."
- Julia Cameron

Scorpio rules the Underworld, and with the Moon in Scorpio, you feel comfortable in the dark, hidden realms. You need your own private Bat Cave for diving into emotional depths, exploring the Mystery, and making magic. Ideally, you should have a creative space that is all your own, even if it's just a screened-off corner of a room, or a diary with a lock. You feel safest when you can work in secret, and may feel especially creative at night.

Fill your space with candles, incense and spiritual or religious images -- whatever helps you connect with magic and mystery. Include red and black, your power colors, to fuel your passion and intensity. You have an affinity with all things occult -- witchcraft,

22

Tarot cards, astrology, the I-Ching -- and these can be excellent resources for tapping into your intuition and inspiring your creativity.

As a Water sign, Scorpionic emotions run deep, and the deeper you go, the more creative you feel. Scorpio is driven to get to the core or essence, to discover profound meaning behind ordinary events and circumstances. Your creative gift is to bring what's hidden into the light, thereby healing and transforming what has been repressed or suppressed. You can maintain your creative inspiration by always following your passions, and engaging in what holds meaning for you.

The intensity of your passion might sometimes seem scary or overwhelming, but suppressing these feelings is a form of creative suicide. Surrendering emotional control, letting your feelings flow, is the key to accessing your deepest levels of creativity. Remember to ask your guides, higher power, and other invisibles for help with staying open, as well as seeking support from loved ones.

When you see yourself as a channel for creative expression, rather than trying to control the process, your creative power is strongest.

In order not to get entirely lost in the darkness and emotional depths, it's helpful to have a daily practice that grounds you in physical reality. This can be as simple as walking, meditation or stretching. To balance your attunement to the Big Questions of life and death, pay attention to the little things you appreciate in your everyday life, perhaps making a list each night of what you're grateful for.

☽ ♐

Moon in Sagittarius
or in the 9th House

"Creativity is a natural extension of our enthusiasm."
- EARL NIGHTINGALE

You don't necessarily require a huge creative space, but you do need the feeling of freedom and openness. Naturally buoyant and optimistic, the only thing that makes you really cranky is feeling restricted. "Don't Fence Me In" could be your theme song.

Fiery Sagittarius is a Centaur -- half-human and half-horse -- and it's the animal in you that needs room to get wild. Spacious and bright environments, images of mountains, forests and wild animals, and objects from nature all connect you with your feral self. Maps, globes and star charts serve as reminders of the great big world out there, inspiring you to create from a place of expansion and higher vision.

While you enjoy the opportunities and diversity of the city, the wilderness feeds your soul. Spending time in nature enhances your instincts and intuition and fuels your creative fire. If you don't live in close proximity to the wild, make sure to take periodic time out of your busy life to get lost in Mother Nature. City parks and paved trails are not sufficient -- you need to be forging your own territory, taking risks and, ideally, crossing borders.

Travel is your lifeblood. Adventures that take you outside your ordinary reality and into exotic locales are essential to sustaining creative inspiration (and general happiness). Mental and spiritual journeys -- consciousness-raising workshops, philosophical exploration, meditative practices -- satisfy your human half's need to expand awareness.

You need to feel like you're always growing and developing. If your creative spirit feels stifled by boredom and routine, it's time to plan your next voyage into the unknown.

Use your visionary and intuitive powers to dream big, but don't be afraid to start small. If you can't immediately quit your job and fly to Paris to satisfy expatriate artist fantasies, find small ways to move toward this goal (e.g., sign up for a painting class, or French lessons). It might take a little while for reality to catch up with your high ideals, but keep the faith. Incorporating your passions into your everyday life, you build your dream step by step.

☽ ♑

Moon in Capricorn
or in the 10th House

"Do not fear mistakes. There are none."
- Miles Davis

If your creative space doesn't look like an executive suite, it should at least function like one. With your Moon in pragmatic Capricorn, you feel and work best in an environment that is organized, systematized, efficient and free of clutter. Even if your outer life hasn't yet caught up with your high ambitions, your creative space should give you a feeling of achievement and success. Surround yourself with items of high quality and lasting value.

Include objects from the natural world to stay connected to the source of your creativity -- Mother Earth. Images of mountains inspire you toward the heights you are here to climb and help you

25

remember your higher vision. To keep from becoming overly rigid, bring a little watery flow into your space, with a small fountain, images of rivers or lakes, or CD's with the sound of waves. Gray, black, and all earth tones help you feel grounded and focused.

To access and stay in the creative flow, you need to keep your heart open. Sensitive by nature, you may protect your emotions behind a projection of cool and in so doing, cut off your connection to the flow. Risk letting down your guard and reveal your vulnerability, a necessity for tapping into your rich reservoir of creativity and enhancing your intuition. Emotional wounds from the past can be used as fuel for creative expression, and through this process, potentially healed.

You feel inspired by success stories, so seek out movies and biographies about creative people you respect and admire who were able to achieve their dreams. Don't get discouraged if it takes a long time to reach your own ambitious goals. Patience, persistence, solitude and self-discipline are your resources. Remember that asking for support when you need it is a sign of strength, not weakness.

Your biggest challenge to creative expression may be making the time for it in the midst of your busy life. Eminently practical by nature, you might see creativity for its own sake as a waste of time, because it doesn't offer immediately tangible results. Or, you might see the value in other people's creative expression, but don't feel worthy of giving that gift to yourself.

You know you're neglecting your inner life and creative needs when you feel like you're "running on empty" and your work in the outer world no longer fulfills you. Make time for dreaming. Commune with nature, and nurture your physical body. Do what you love, and trust that when you follow your creative passions, they will bring you closer to your true destination.

Moon in Aquarius
or in the 11th House

"We will discover the nature of our particular genius when we stop trying to conform to our own and other people's models, learn to be ourselves and allow our natural channel to open."

— SHAKTI GAWAIN

What feels nurturing and safe to you might look very different from conventional concepts. Aquarius, sign of the scientist, inventor and rebel, infuses the watery Moon with a strong dose of intellect, logic and eccentricity.

The kind of space you need to access and sustain your creativity might seem just plain weird to other people, and for you, the weirder the better. Pee Wee's Playhouse can serve as your inspiration. You need to be surrounded by books, electronics, inventions, art, ideas and people that stimulate your mind and expand your consciousness. You might need to make frequent changes in your space -- rearranging furniture, throwing out what no longer excites you, and bringing in new toys.

If you set up your space according to other people's ideas of what it should look like, you'll feel trapped and depressed. You need to express the truth of who you are, and your space should reflect your unconventional and rebellious nature. Your ideal creative space makes you feel free and open to possibility, so it should have large windows and high ceilings. Aquarius is an Air sign -- you should feel like you can spread your wings and take flight.

Sources of creative inspiration include science and science fiction, technology, all things futuristic and strange, and humanitarian causes. Look to your outrageous, rebellious and eccentric family members and ancestors for support in expressing your own originality. (You might have to dig through the skeletons in the family closet to find them.)

Your friendships and community can also provide significant sustenance. You are learning to strike a balance between nurturing others' creativity, and receiving support for your own efforts. The more you value your unique creative vision, and are willing to reveal your inner truth, the more able you are to manifest your high ideals in the world.

You can heighten your intuition by letting your emotions flow freely and connecting with your playful side. You may have a tendency to be overly serious, to intellectualize your feelings, or shut down instincts that seem too wild or illogical. Directly experiencing the power of your emotions may make you feel vulnerable and uncomfortable, but it enables you to connect more easily with your instincts and imagination, and create from a deeper level.

Moon in Pisces
or in the 12th House

"I dream a lot. I do more painting when I'm not painting. It's in the subconscious."
- ANDREW WYETH

Your creative space should feel like your very own Fantasy Island -- magical, mystical, and existing in an alternate universe. With your Moon in dreamy, psychedelic Pisces, your creativity flourishes in an environment that inspires a feeling of infinite possibility.

An island is actually an ideal creative setting for you, both literally and metaphorically. Pisces the Fish feels at home in and around water, and is creatively inspired by the ocean. If you're not living on an actual island, include oceanic reminders in your space -- blues and greens, rocks and shells collected from the beach, and images of mermaids, fish, and the sea. Listen to recordings of ocean waves -- and at least occasionally, if possible, hear a live performance -- to connect with the creative flow.

While you thrive on sampling a variety of life experiences and connecting with diverse people, you also require periods of solitude, a metaphorical retreat to your private island. Because you easily absorb the thoughts and feelings of people around you, you need time alone to decompress and get in touch with your own imagination and vision. Trust your feelings to let you know when you're going overboard in the opposite direction and isolating to your detriment.

You can enhance your creativity and intuition by paying attention to your dreams. They reveal important information about the needs of your creative spirit. Before you go to sleep, ask for a dream to give you guidance or information about a situation in your waking life. Write what you remember when you wake up. Writing down your dreams alerts your subconscious that you are paying attention, and your intuition increases accordingly.

Your creative gift is the ability to tap into the collective unconscious, through your dreams and imagination, and then bring forth the vision you find there. Your creative expression could take many forms, but you might especially feel an affinity for music, dance, poetry, acting and painting. Having a simple daily practice (walking, meditating, writing in a journal) helps you come back to Earth after exploring these ethereal realms.

Venus

Seducing the Muse

"Let the beauty we love be what we do."
– RUMI

Venus, Goddess of Love and Beauty, was also patroness of culture and the arts in the Roman pantheon. Astrologically, you can think of Venus as your inner muse, the part of you that inspires and supports your artist self. This creative goddess requires seduction, and her sign reveals how your particular muse would like to be called forth.

In her dominion over the realm of love, Venus ultimately represents self-love, a necessary ingredient in the creative process. Venus's sign can help you identify any blocks around loving and valuing yourself enough to express your creativity. Additionally, Venus's sign reveals your innate creative talents.

Venus in Aries
or in the 1st House

*"You can't wait for inspiration, you
have to go after it with a club."*
                                    - JACK LONDON

Imagine your Venus in Aries Muse as Xena the Woman Warrior. Approach your creative life as a heroic adventure, and your Muse will supply a steady surge of inspiration. Once you jump into the creative fire, she'll arrive on the scene ready for battle.

Novelty and risk-taking get your Muse's attention. As the first sign of the Zodiac, Aries needs to go first, to pioneer uncharted territory. Creatively, this means having the courage to step outside your comfort zone and try something new, whether approaching your art with a fresh perspective, or experimenting with a new form of expression. Let your excitement and enthusiasm guide you toward the next creative challenge.

You strengthen your self-worth by following your instincts and passions. When you identify what you truly desire and take action toward fulfilling your dream, you send a clear message to your subconscious that you value yourself. Releasing judgment and viewing life through innocent eyes ensures your continued inspiration.

Aries rules the eyes, giving you a talent for creative vision, and for the visual arts. Your gift for leadership might find expression through directing or producing, while the Warrior in you might be drawn to athletic arts, like dancing or Contact Improvisation.

♀ ♉

Venus in Taurus
or in the 2nd House

*"Poetry is about slowing down.... It's about reading the
same thing again and again, really savoring it, living
inside the poem. There's no rush to find out what
happens in a poem. It's really about feeling
one syllable rubbing against another, one
word giving way to another, and sensing the
justice of that relationship between one
word, the next, the next, the next."*

- MARK STRAND

Relax. Slow down. And pay attention. Your Venus in Taurus muse magically appears when you are attuned to the beauty and perfection of the present moment. She likes to feel serene, secure and comfortable, and evoking these feelings in yourself is the best way to invite her inspiration.

Your Muse responds well to routine, so establish a simple ritual for calling her in, like lighting a candle, taking ten deep breaths, or meditating for five minutes. Start your invocation of the Muse with a prayer of gratitude, acknowledging all that you are genuinely thankful for in this moment.

The surest route to strengthening your self-worth is by nurturing your body. Establishing and maintaining daily self-care routines sends a clear message to your subconscious that you value yourself. The more worthy and loved you feel, the more your creativity flows. Imagine that your Muse resides within your physical being, and that to support your creativity you need to take excellent care of your body.

As Venus rules Taurus, and is therefore strong in this sign, you are

32

likely to be blessed with many creative talents. Because Taurus governs the throat, you may be especially drawn to singing. Or, because Taurus connects you with the Earth's rhythms, drumming, dancing and other ways of keeping the beat may serve your creative process. Your pragmatism gives you an affinity for utilitarian, earthy crafts, like pottery, carpentry and gardening.

♀ ♊

Venus in Gemini
or in the 3rd House

"Around here, however, we don't look backwards
for very long. We keep moving forward, opening
up new doors and doing new things, because
we're curious… and curiosity keeps
leading us down new paths."

- WALT DISNEY

Your Venus in Gemini Muse is brainy, speedy and multi-dimensional. Air is her element, and she loves to fly around following whatever catches her curiosity. Imagine her as a fairy, butterfly, hummingbird or Peter Pan -- or as all of the above, depending on the moment. Ruled by mercurial Mercury, your Muse is a shape-shifter, likely to appear in diverse forms.

To keep your Muse interested (she gets bored easily), offer her variety, mental stimulation, and new realms to explore. Entice her with trips to the library, classes and workshops, and journeys to unfamiliar destinations. Balance your need for social stimulation with time out for sifting through and processing all the information you've taken in. Without these occasional periods of solitude, you lose sight of your unique creative vision.

When you speak your truth, you send a clear message to your subconscious that you love and value yourself. Harness the power of your sharp mind by noticing what you tell yourself about your creativity, and consciously choose to say only positive and supportive statements about yourself, as if you were encouraging a good friend.

You have a talent for connecting disparate ideas and people, opening minds, and inspiring curiosity, wonder and humor. These talents might find expression through the communication arts -- writing, reporting, filmmaking, public speaking and broadcasting. As Gemini rules the hands and fingers, you may also have an affinity for stringed instruments or the piano.

Venus in Cancer
or in the 4th House

"The great thing about this kind of work is that every feeling that you have, every negative feeling, is in a way precious. It is your building material, it's your stone, it's something you use to build your work.... Don't duck pain. It's precious, it's your gold mine, it's the gold in your mine."
    - MADELEINE L'ENGLE

If you want your Venus in Cancer Muse to come out and play, you'll have to convince her it's safe. Cancer the Crab wears a tough protective shield for a very good reason -- she's sensitive, vulnerable, and afraid of being eaten alive. Entice your Muse out of her shell with a dreamy and comfortable setting, soft music, and a plate of homemade cookies. Once she feels nurtured and secure, she'll reward you with flowing inspiration.

Your lunar-ruled Muse speaks to you through your intuition and dreams. You may feel her presence most powerfully late at night, especially under a Full Moon (when she needs to howl). Your Muse shape-shifts according to the phases of the Moon, and riding the emotional tides is a pre-requisite for tapping into the creative well.

You can strengthen your self-worth by tuning into and honoring your feelings. Remember that creative expression can emerge from all emotional states. Don't neglect your creativity by waiting until you feel "inspired," just start where you are.

Your sensitivity and compassion are valuable creative resources. You have the ability to feel your way into different characters, giving you a talent for acting or writing fiction. You also have a gift for creating beautiful and nurturing environments, and may be drawn to interior decorating, architecture or landscape design. Gardening, cooking and baking are other forms of expression through which you creatively nourish yourself and others.

Venus in Leo
or in the 5th House

"The thing about writers that people don't realize
is that a lot of what they do is play. You know,
playing around with. That doesn't mean that it

*isn't serious or that it doesn't have a serious
meaning or a serious intention."*
- MARGARET ATWOOD

Your Muse appreciates, and may demand, the royal treatment. Leo the Lion is king of the jungle, and your Venus in Leo Muse longs to be queen, or at least head diva. Present her with a bouquet of sunflowers (Leo is ruled by the Sun) and lavish treats (as expensive as you can reasonably afford). When your Muse feels appropriately worshiped and romanced, she'll reward you by shining her bright light of inspiration.

Leo rules the heart, and your Muse is enthused when you create from love -- love for yourself, your art, and your present or future audience. You know you're expressing yourself from the heart when you feel on fire and in the flow.

If you're feeling disconnected from your heart (and your Muse), take time to identify what feels like fun to you. Incorporating more of these joyful elements into your life feeds your inspiration.

Having fun brings you into the present moment, a highly creative state of being where anything is possible. Balance your attunement to the present moment with occasional thoughts about your long-range vision for your creative life. Don't be afraid to dream big, and then return to the present, to what you love, trusting that your heart will lead you exactly where you need to go.

Naturally gifted in many areas, your creative expression may take a variety of forms. With your affinity for drama, you have a talent for all aspects of the theater -- directing, producing, writing and performing. You excel in leadership roles, where you can put your unique stamp on whatever you create.

♀ ♍

Venus in Virgo
or in the 6th House

*"Every morning between 9:00 and 12:00 I go to my
room and sit before a piece of paper. Many
times, I just sit for three hours with no ideas
coming to me. But I know one thing. If an
idea does come between 9:00 and 12:00,
I am there ready for it."*

- FLANNERY O'CONNOR

Keep it simple. Your Venus in Virgo Muse will not be impressed by sentimentality, drama or expensive gifts. You can get her attention by cleaning and organizing your creative space, and showing up ready to work at a regularly scheduled time. When you prove to your Muse that you're serious about your creativity, she'll arrive on the scene with abundant inspiration.

Virgo represents the archetype of the Virgin, but please don't picture your Muse her as a frumpy spinster. The original meaning of Virgo denotes self-possession and sovereignty, not chastity. This Muse is independent, exacting, and holds high standards. Virgo seeks purity in the sense of simplifying and peeling away the layers until all that's left is the core or essence. She wants her creative expression to be maximally useful, productive and of service.

You can strengthen your self-love and self-worth by releasing perfectionism and accepting yourself and your creative expression exactly as is. Don't delay offering your artistic gifts because you judge them to be imperfect. You perfect your gifts through practice, which means taking the risk of starting where you are, and having faith that you'll develop the skills you need along the way. Balance your natural tendency toward criticism with consciously noting everything that is perfect in your life right now.

Ruled by Mercury the Messenger God, Virgo has a gift for writing, reporting, editing and broadcasting. Your attention to detail and ability to extrapolate an understanding of the whole by analyzing one small part give you a talent for research and investigation. Because of your earthy pragmatism, you may also have an affinity for creative endeavors with practical applications -- gardening, baking, pottery, knitting and all crafts.

Venus in Libra
or in the 7th House

"I don't know the key to success, but the key to
failure is trying to please everybody."

- BILL COSBY

A sucker for romance, your Venus in Libra Muse delights in flowers, candlelight and chocolate. She is drawn to elegant, serene and orderly settings, and beauty in all manifestations. If you treat her right (i.e., indulgently), she will shower you with inspiration.

Libra's symbol is the Scales, and your Muse requires balance and harmony for optimal performance. If you feel out of balance in any area of life, your creativity will wither, and your Muse will wait until the Scales return to equilibrium before gracing you with her presence. Often, you may find you've put so much energy into your relationships that you've neglected your own needs. Taking time for yourself provides the necessary recalibration.

You strengthen your self-worth by acting on your desires rather than trying to please others. Discover your true creative passion by going within and identifying what excites you. Your analytical mind will want to weigh all the options and possible outcomes before taking action, but over-thinking can sabotage the creative process. At some point you have to risk doing something, and trust that your intuition will guide you in the right direction.

Venus is at home in Libra, and you are blessed with many creative talents. Your eye (and ear) for balance, beauty and harmony could find expression in the visual arts, writing or music. In addition to your own artistic gifts, you also have the ability to recognize and promote other people's talents, perhaps as an agent, editor, publisher or publicist.

Venus in Scorpio
or in the 8th House

"Writers write about what obsesses them.... When I'm writing, the darkness is always there. I go where the pain is."
- ANNE RICE

Your Venus in Scorpio Muse is likely to appear after dark, and not always in the most respectable locations. Scorpio rules the Underworld -- all things hidden, mysterious and taboo. When you're committed to diving into the darkness, the depths and the Mystery, your Muse will meet you there with abundant inspiration.

Superficiality bores her. Your Muse is interested in Life's big questions: Why are we here? What really matters? How can we survive day to day knowing we could die at any moment? (Yes, she can be a little morbid.) Courage, stamina and perseverance are your creative resources as you explore the unknown and journey to the core of existence through your art.

Get your Muse's attention with ritual and magic. Light red or black candles, say a simple prayer, pick a Tarot card, or throw the I-Ching. Making connections between physical reality and subconscious realms -- seeing the deeper meaning behind everyday circumstances -- heightens your creativity.

Your creative gift is to reveal the beauty of what has been hidden or repressed, and to remind people what has true value and meaning. You may be drawn to exploring taboo subjects through your art -- sex, death -- and anything that makes people uncomfortable. This process of excavation and transformation might happen through writing, or the magical or healing arts. Mysteries, thrillers, conspiracies, secrets and the occult are your creative domain.

Venus in Sagittarius
or in the 9th House

"No manipulation is possible in a work of art,
but every miracle is. Those artists who
dabble in eternity, or who aim to never
manipulate but only to lay out hard

truths, grow accustomed
to miracles."
- ANNIE DILLARD

Your Venus in Sagittarius muse will not be seduced with candlelight, soft music and a bouquet of pretty flowers. You'll have better luck with a bonfire, heavy metal and an expanse of wilderness. Sagittarius is the sign of the adventurer, globe trotter, philosopher and outlaw. As a Centaur (half-human, half-horse), Sagittarius is not entirely tame or civilized, so to find your muse you'll have to be willing to get wild. She appreciates adventure, spontaneity, and journeys to exotic locales.

When you can't get into the wilderness or out of town, you can appease the Muse with mind-expanding philosophical or spiritual explorations, foreign movies and media -- and by planning your next adventure. She needs something to look forward to that will take her out of the daily grind. Sometimes just going for a walk or run can shift your energy and call back the Muse, who likes to be on the go.

Strengthen your self-love and self-worth by cultivating your higher mind, inner truth, vision and intuition. You develop your faith in the universe by acting on intuitive hunches. Trust that there are invisible forces on your side, supporting you in moving toward your highest good. Pay attention to what you feel grateful for in your life right now, so you can appreciate the present while pursuing your dreams for the future.

You have a talent for inspiring others with your expansive worldview, higher vision and playful humor. Your own willingness to break through boundaries can help free others from limiting beliefs. How exactly these talents are put forth into the world depends on other planets in your chart (see the Sun and Mars), but you are likely to have an affinity for storytelling and the visual arts.

♀ ♑

Venus in Capricorn
or in the 10th House

"Inspiration exists, but it has to find you working."

- PABLO PICASSO

You'll have to work hard to get your Venus in Capricorn Muse to come out and play. Ruled by Saturn, the cosmic taskmaster, she holds high standards, and demands discipline, respect and perseverance. She wants to see that you're committed to your creative goals. Only then will she arrive on the scene with abundant inspiration.

Call in your exacting Muse by offering a clean, well-organized setting and the best art supplies you can reasonably afford. Schedule dates with your Muse—and show up on time and ready to work. While these outer actions are important, the most significant key to attracting your Muse is passion. Once you've identified your creative ambition, and believe in your ability to climb toward it, your Muse will happily accompany you all the way to the top.

Strengthen your self-worth by taking small, practical steps toward manifesting your dreams. Don't let perfectionism or fear of failure keep you from simply moving step by step toward your goals, while staying focused on your higher vision. You require periods of solitude to clarify your goals and recharge your creative batteries.

Capricorn is a pragmatic Earth sign, and you may be drawn to artistic outlets with tangible, practical results, like carpentry and building, gardening and plant medicine, and the culinary arts. You also have a talent for creating systems and structures, such as organizations, businesses or empires. Your sense of humor is a valuable creative resource.

Venus in Aquarius
or in the 11th House

"I can't understand why people are frightened of new ideas. I'm frightened of the old ones."

\- JOHN CAGE

Your Venus in Aquarius Muse is a free spirit and a rebel. You can get her attention by breaking convention, planning a revolution, or simply doing what makes you feel liberated. She becomes especially interested when you use your creative gifts to serve the greater good or a higher mission. Idealistic and humanitarian Aquarius is the Water Bearer, bringing consciousness and enlightenment to the world.

Always ahead of her time, your Muse delights in futuristic gadgets and technology. She lives in the realm of science fiction, and you can reach her by opening your mind to galaxies far far away. Further stimulate your creativity by socializing with people who espouse eccentric ideas and broaden your perspective.

You strengthen your self-worth by taking action toward manifesting your high ideals. Your mind might get so caught up in idealistic visions of how things should be that you overlook the possibilities of the present moment. Risk jumping in and doing something to build faith in yourself and in humanity.

Remember to have fun in the process, and not take yourself too seriously.

A logical Air sign, Aquarius has a natural talent for scientific and technological creative endeavors. Your gifts of accurate perception and seeing a higher perspective might find expression through writing. You may also be drawn to various forms of media as a means of sharing your vision with a wide audience.

Venus in Pisces
or in the 12th House

"Put your ear down close to your soul and listen hard."
- ANNE SEXTON

Imagine your Venus in Pisces Muse as a mermaid -- magical, mystical, and at home in the water. If you can't get to the coast to find her, call her in with a salty bath, the sound of ocean waves, and plenty of dream time. She needs to escape ordinary reality and access alternate dimensions.

Your Muse is likely to speak to you through your dreams, or when you're deeply relaxed. Meditation, yoga and dance are possible ways to alter your consciousness so you can reach the Muse. The more you are willing to surrender to the flow, and follow your feelings and intuition, the more inspired you feel.

Strengthen your self-worth by cultivating your connection with Spirit and the invisible realms. The divinatory arts (Tarot, the

I-Ching, astrology) can help you bridge ordinary reality with the unconscious.

In traditional astrology, Venus is considered exalted -- reaching her highest expression -- in the sign of the Fish. You are blessed with multiple creative talents, and may shift between different forms of expression as the spirit moves you. Your gift for helping people transcend ordinary reality and come closer to the divine might find expression through music, film or fiction. When you create from the deepest levels of emotional truth, your art is truly inspirational.

Masculine Creativity

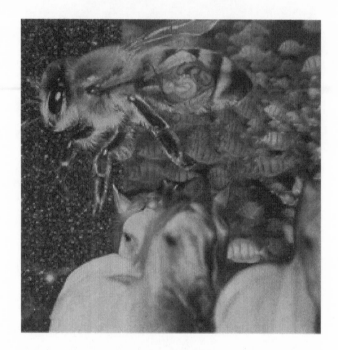

The Sun and Mars

☉ ♂

"Whatever you can do or dream you can, begin it;
boldness has genius, power and magic in it."

- JOHANN WOLFGANG GOETHE

You've set your space and seduced your muse. . . Now what? The next step in the creative process requires taking that big leap of faith -- the first brushstroke of color on a blank canvas, the first words typed on an empty screen, the first note played or sung. . .

Inevitably, this stage of the process invokes some degree of fear and anxiety because you're heading into unknown territory. The masculine creative planets, the Sun and Mars, offer guidance for developing courage, stoking your passion, and expressing your authentic self.

☉ The Sun

Shining Your Light

*"There is a vitality, a life force, a quickening that is
translated through you into action, and there is only
one of you in all time, this expression is unique,
and if you block it, it will never exist through
any other medium; and be lost.... It is not your
business to determine how good it is.... It is
your business to keep it yours clearly and
directly, to keep the channel open."*

         - MARTHA GRAHAM

The Sun is perhaps the easiest astrological "planet" to understand. Just as all life on Earth depends on the Sun for its existence, the astrological Sun represents your own creative life force, the battery pack you can plug into to recharge your vitality. When you lose connection or fail to express your Sun, you feel joyless and lackluster, like a wilting plant too long deprived of light.

Your Sun sign reveals how you shine your light -- how you project your unique self into the world. Additionally, it shows the creative risks you need to take to develop a strong sense of self, to feel fulfilled and happy. Many have made the analogy between your inner artist and your inner child. The Sun signifies both archetypes, reminding us of the playful side of creativity. Your Sun sign indicates how to please your inner artist-child, by cultivating the art of fun.

Sun in Aries
or in the 1st House

"If you're not failing every now and again, it's a sign you're not doing anything very innovative."
- WOODY ALLEN

As the first sign of the Zodiac, Aries provides the creative spark that sets the whole cycle into motion. You are a pioneer, trailblazer and innovator. When you follow your excitement, your enthusiasm becomes contagious, and you inspire others to pursue their own creative dreams.

In traditional astrology the Sun is considered exalted -- reaching its highest expression -- in the sign of the Ram. Perhaps more than any other sign, you require a creative outlet, a channel for expressing your intense fiery energy.

Aries represents the archetype of the Warrior, and your creativity shines brightest when you take on heroic challenges. You need opportunities for proving your strength, courage and stamina. Without a battle to fight, you feel bored and restless.

The Fool is another Aries archetype, representing the innocence and naiveté required to initiate a new cycle. Your creative risk is to always approach your life from a fresh perspective, open to whatever the Universe has to offer. As you leap into unknown creative territory, let your feelings and gut instincts guide you, rather than past experiences or your rational mind. Your actions might not make sense and may even seem foolish, but trust your intuition to take you in the right direction. Falling victim to judgment, skepticism or cynicism cuts you off from the child within and from your creative inspiration.

You might work well in short bursts of intense and all-consuming creative activity. To sustain your creative life long-term, you may need to cultivate patience and balance. Incorporate exercise into your daily routine (especially martial arts), and practices that help you feel peaceful and centered. Although you may prefer working independently, from time to time you can benefit from creative input from others, and working in partnership.

Your creative energy might find expression in various forms throughout your life. It is essential that you follow your desires, interests and passions, even if that path involves frequent changes. Because Aries is ruled by Mars, pay special attention to your Mars sign (described in the next chapter) for clues as to how to channel your creative energy.

Famous Aries Creators: ARETHA FRANKLIN, BILLIE HOLIDAY, DAVID LETTERMAN, EDDIE MURPHY, EUDORA WELTY, FRANCIS FORD COPPOLA, HOLLY HUNTER, LEONARDO DA VINCI, MAYA ANGELOU, VINCENT VAN GOGH

Sun in Taurus
or in the 2nd House

"Accept yourself as an artist, and consider your task to be simply expressing what you see in your own voice. You don't have to prove anything to anybody."

— PAT SCHNEIDER

Your creative energy is needed to generate abundance, stability, beauty and planetary consciousness. Taurus the Bull signifies the archetype of the builder, the farmer, and the Earth spirit. Ruled by Venus, you're blessed with a bounty of creative gifts, which could find expression in multiple forms. Pay special attention to Venus's sign for clues to creative talents.

Your creative passion arises from states of deep stillness and inner silence. Enjoying nature and communing with plants and animals help you drop into that quiet place, and get in touch with what has meaning and value for you. Balance your pragmatic focus on the material world with time for tuning into your deepest emotions and the invisible realm of Spirit. Your connection with invisible forces (especially the fairies, devas and other nature spirits) can provide valuable support for your creative expression.

51

Though you have a self-reliant streak and might generally work best on your own, be open to periodic creative brainstorming with others. Accepting assistance in the form of ideas, inspiration or material resources is not a sign of weakness, but rather another expression of your innate resourcefulness. Thinking you have to do it all on your own limits your creative opportunities and can leave you feeling lonely and burdened.

Though you may be slow getting started, once you commit to a course of action you're a relentless worker. Your famous Bull-headed stubbornness serves your creativity by giving you the stamina to persevere and follow through on creative projects.

However, inflexibility can also result in creative stagnation. If you feel like you're in a rut, you might be doing the same thing over and over, expecting different results. Take the risk of releasing the old ways and try something new, and you'll be rewarded with an influx of fresh creative energy.

As an Earth sign, you might be drawn to working with clay and other natural materials, or to practical arts and crafts, like gardening, cooking and knitting. Carpentry and other forms of building are other likely creative outlets. As Taurus rules the throat, you have a talent for singing, and your connection with Earth's rhythms gives you an affinity for drumming, dancing and playing bass.

Famous Taurus Creators: CHARLES MINGUS, CHARLOTTE BRONTE, CHER, DAVID BYRNE, ELLA FITZGERALD, GEORGE LUCAS, JACK JOHNSON, MARTHA GRAHAM, SALVADOR DALI, UMA THURMAN

☉ ♊

Sun in Gemini
or in the 3rd House

"It is the function of art to renew our perception.
What we are familiar with we cease to see.
The writer shakes up the familiar
scene, and, as if by magic, we
see a new meaning in it."

— ANAÏS NIN

Your creative energy opens minds, inspiring wonder, curiosity and a sense of possibility. Ruled by Mercury -- the fast-moving Messenger God -- Gemini is the cosmic communicator, connecting diverse people, ideas and cultures. Your role is to sample a vast variety of experiences and perspectives, comprehend the deeper correlations between disparate themes, and share your message with the world.

The famous duality of the Twins could show up in your creative life as pursuing more than one form of artistic expression. Multifaceted and multiply talented, your curiosity draws you in many different directions, and you feel fired up when you encounter the new. Travel, classes and workshops, stimulating conversations, and trips to the library or bookstore recharge your creative energy.

While you thrive on social encounters and mental expansion, you also require periods of solitude and reflection. If you are over-connected, constantly attached to your cell phone, television, radio, Ipod or Ipad, you will lose touch with your creative source. Unplugging from external sources of information enables you to discover your inner truth and clarify your message.

Expressing your unique thoughts and feelings requires taking a creative risk. You might be afraid that people won't like or accept you, or that you'll be seen as stupid or wrong. You might be afraid to commit to an idea or belief, knowing it's likely to change.

Your challenge is to identify and communicate what you think and feel in this moment, trusting that honestly expressing that truth will serve the greater good. You don't have to have all the answers or information before you speak (write, paint, play music...), just start with what is currently flowing through your mind and heart.

Delight your inner artist-child with "what if" games, where you marvel at the limitless possibilities of our magical world.

A natural storyteller, you may be drawn to writing, researching, reporting and broadcasting. Your gift for mimicry and ability to access multiple personalities could find expression in acting or stand-up comedy. You might also have an affinity for music, especially woodwind and stringed instruments.

Famous Gemini Creators: ALLEN GINSBERG, ANGELINA JOLIE, BOB DYLAN, ISADORA DUNCAN, JOAN RIVERS, JOHNNY DEPP, JOYCE CAROL OATES, MELISSA ETHERIDGE, MILES DAVIS, PRINCE

Sun in Cancer
or in the 4th House

"Creation is never about changing yourself; it is about meeting yourself, probing deep into your own core. Creation wants only to fulfill your deepest desire:

*to know and accept yourself as you are.... You go
into what is there, you discover the courage to
face what exists. You step into the middle of
yourself and move from there."*

- MICHELE CASSOU & STEWART CUBLEY

Your healing creative energy nurtures and sustains life, and inspires people to feel the depths of emotion. Cancer the Crab represents the Great Mother, the all-powerful creator goddess. Ruled by the ever-changing Moon, Cancer relates to all phases of waxing and waning, from the introspective dark of the Moon to the rowdy celebration of her fullness.

Your sensitivity is your greatest creative resource. With the ability to feel what others feel, and tap into the deep well of your own psyche, there is no limit to your imagination. Your emotions shift with the phases of the Moon, and your creativity is strongest when you give yourself permission to connect with and express the vast spectrum of your feelings, without judgment.

You need a creative outlet that satisfies your rich inner life and allows you to use your imagination and sensitivity in a positive way. Without such opportunities for expression, you can get stuck in the famous Cancerian crabbiness.

Like the Crab who periodically sheds her shell, your creative risk is to let go of what you have outgrown in order to move toward what you really want. When you hold onto anything that has outlived its purpose -- beliefs, possessions, habits, jobs, relationships -- your creativity suffers. Your acute intuition tells you (possibly through your belly) when it's time to let go. Although you may fear losing security and safety by releasing the old, the creative energy that rushes in when you take that risk actually provides greater internal security in the long run.

You can recharge your creative batteries by taking time to

nurture yourself and your creative projects. Mother to the world, your challenge is to give equal time to yourself, tending to your creative passions as you would to your own child. Beware of using your natural tendency to nurture others as an excuse not to move toward your own creative goals. Ultimately, you are more effective at nurturing others when you are also taking care of your own needs.

Your inner artist-child has a bit of a loony streak (especially under a Full Moon), delighting in the ridiculous and absurd. Maintaining a sense of humor, no matter what emotional state you're currently experiencing, keeps you in touch with this playful side of yourself.

Home, homeland, family, ancestors, memory, and the past are themes you might explore through your creative work. Your ability to feel what others are feeling can be channeled into creating believable characters through acting or writing. You have a gift for acquiring and building resources that could be channeled into nurturing and growing a business or non-profit organization.

Famous Cancer Creators: ANDREW WYETH, ANJELICA HUSTON, BECK, BILL COSBY, FRANCES MCDORMAND, FRIDA KAHLO, GILDA RADNER, HARRISON FORD, JACK WHITE, MERYL STREEP

Sun in Leo
or in the 5th House

*"There's room for everybody on the planet
to be creative and conscious if you are*

your own person. If you're trying to be
like somebody else, then there isn't."

- TORI AMOS

The Sun is at home in the sign of the Lion, endowing you with courage, confidence, and an abundance of creative gifts. Your dazzling creative energy brings more light and love to the planet. As king or queen of the jungle, you long to be a leader and a star, recognized and appreciated for your uniqueness.

Your greatest creative resource is your generous heart -- the part of the body ruled by Leo. The heart, like the proverbial parachute, works best when open. Identify the activities that help you feel more open-hearted and consciously incorporate more of these elements into your life. When you express yourself from the heart, you feel a steady flow of creative inspiration, and at the same time inspire others to open their hearts.

The need for attention and approval can block the creative flow because it takes you into your mind and out of your heart, as well as into the future and out of the present moment. Your creative risk is to let go of other people's opinions and freely share your authentic thoughts and feelings -- to simply be yourself.

Don't get tricked into thinking that you are the source of your talent or creativity. The Sun is your source, and your creativity shines brightest when you are simply a channel for the light.

As Leo signifies the archetype of the child, you have an innate ability to access a childlike state of being. Children possess the gift of innocence, seeing the world from a fresh perspective and open to all possibilities. Before they are taught "right" and "wrong" ways of creating, children express themselves unselfconsciously, honestly revealing however they feel in the moment. Cultivating innocence and wonder, acting on the impulses of your heart, and having fun are ways to return to this highly creative childlike state.

Although you are likely to possess creative talent in many areas, your love of drama gives you a special affinity for all aspects of theater and film -- performing, directing, producing and writing. Your talent for leadership might find expression through teaching, especially working with children.

Famous Leo Creators: ANDY WARHOL, CHARLIZE THERON, COCO CHANEL, JAMES BALDWIN, JERRY GARCIA, MADONNA, MICK JAGGER, SEAN PENN, TORI AMOS, WHITNEY HOUSTON

Sun in Virgo
or in the 6th House

"Making the simple complicated is commonplace; making the complicated simple, awesomely simple, that's creativity."

- CHARLES MINGUS

Your creative energy is needed to simplify, distill, organize and heal. Virgo the Virgin signifies purity, rather than inexperience. Your role is to clear away the excess and see through to the core or essence.

Applying your gifts of accurate perception and attention to detail, you serve the greater good by alerting people to what's truly important, what needs to be done, and what needs to be released. In its highest expression, Virgo inspires others to notice the beauty and perfection of the present moment, revealing the divine in everyday circumstances.

Don't wait until you, your environment, and everyone in your life are in perfect order before you start fulfilling your dreams. Your creative risk is to start where you are, with the materials and skills at hand. See yourself and your creative expression as ever-evolving works-in-progress, giving yourself permission to make mistakes, just like ordinary humans. Self-love, self-acceptance and humility enable you to contribute your gifts and talents right now. The more you utilize your skills, the more inspired you feel.

Perfectionism can lead to insecurity and negativity, which dampen your creative fire. Virgo Stephen King threw his first novel into the trash, ready to surrender his dream of being a writer. His wife rescued the book, Carrie, which became the first of many bestsellers. Recognize that you are your own worst critic, and trust that your work has beauty and value, even if you can't see it right now. Find friends or mentors who can support you in your creative process, remind you of your brilliance, and let you know when you're being too hard on yourself.

With your serious outlook and endless to-do list, you might routinely neglect your inner child. Schedule playtime into your planner, making dates for what seems fun, silly, or even frivolous. You recharge your creative batteries by reconnecting with the child within, and balancing doing with time for simply being. You are ultimately more productive -- and of greater service -- when you let yourself relax and have fun.

Ruled by Mercury the Messenger God, writing, editing and publishing are natural creative outlets. Your earthy pragmatic spirit enjoys crafty pursuits with practical applications, like gardening, cooking, knitting, carpentry and ceramics. You also have a gift for comedy because of your excellent timing and accurate perception.

Famous Virgo Creators: AGATHA CHRISTIE, CAMERON DIAZ, GRANDMA MOSES, JACK BLACK, JOAN JETT, JOHN CAGE, LEO TOLSTOY, LILY TOMLIN, MICHAEL JACKSON, PETER SELLERS

Sun in Libra
or in the 7th House

"When I am working on a problem I never think about beauty.
I only think about how to solve the problem. But when
I have finished, if the solution is not beautiful,
I know it is wrong."
- BUCKMINSTER FULLER

Your creative energy brings more peace, justice, love and beauty into the world. Like Libra's symbol, the Scales, you seek balance, and the more you experience internal harmony, the more harmony you create in the outer world. Creative expression can be a great resource in your journey to inner peace.

Ruled by Venus, the Goddess of Love, when you do what you love your creativity explodes. In order to discover your creative passion, you might need to spend time in solitude, which helps you access your instincts. Rather than trying to reach a logical conclusion by analyzing all the options, drop into your body and feel what would truly bring you joy. Endless analysis and indecision drain your creativity, and if you get stuck in that mode, you may fail to take action. As soon as you make a decision, you're back in the creative flow.

In your quest for peace, you might strive to please others, which dampens the creative fire. Your creative risk is to commit to and act on your desires, even if you think others might not approve. In making time for your creativity, you might need to develop stronger boundaries with people in your life. Carving out time free of obligations to others isn't selfish, it's necessary. Consider that you'll generate greater harmony in the long run if you honestly express your needs and desires in the present.

To connect with the child within, you need to make a conscious effort to turn off your analytical brain and drop into your heart. Identify what feels like fun to you, and schedule play dates into your calendar. Your inner child might especially enjoy trips to museums or art galleries, movies, concerts, and other ways of interacting with the wider creative culture. Play brings you into the present moment, a powerful place from which to create.

Your natural sense of aesthetics -- the ability to perceive and create balance and beauty -- could find expression through many outlets. You might be drawn to music, writing, painting, photography or design. Your sensitivity and intuitive understanding of how other people experience reality can be utilized in acting or in writing fiction. You work well in collaborations, though you might need to be alone at the beginning of creative projects so you can more easily tap into your intuition.

Famous Libra Creators: ANI DIFRANCO, ANNE RICE, BRUCE SPRINGSTEEN, CHRISTOPHER REEVE, JOHN LENNON, JULIE ANDREWS, SIGOURNEY WEAVER, STING, SUSAN SARANDON, TRUMAN CAPOTE

Sun in Scorpio
or in the 8th House

*"The best art risks most deeply.... It descends into the
subterranean the shameful, the fraught, the urgent
and covert. What could not be said aloud because
it defies conversation. . . What passes invisibly
over the earth because you have not
yet pointed a finger at it."*

- BONNIE FRIEDMAN

Your creative energy is needed to heal, transform and regenerate. In the sign of the Scorpion, the Sun shines into the darkness, revealing what is hidden beneath the surface. You are here to break taboos, explore the mysteries of life, and expose the very core. Your creative path entails transformation at the deepest levels, both for you, by going through the process, and for your audience.

As a Water sign, you live in the emotions, following your feelings and instincts rather than reason or intellect. Scorpio has a reputation for being intense, and for good reason. Although you don't like to show it, you feel deeply and are extremely sensitive. Your creativity flourishes when you reveal your vulnerability, exploring and expressing your deepest emotional truths. Feeling your feelings, in all their intensity (no matter how terrifying) requires courage, strength and stamina -- your creative resources.

When you risk releasing control in the creative process, you're able to tap into a deeper and more powerful creative source. Seeing yourself as an open channel, rather than the sole originator of your creations, helps you access the power of the invisible. Consciously connecting with this realm -- through psychological exploration, mythology, meditation, magic or spirituality

-- enhances your trust in the Universe, making it easier to let go of control.

Avoid burnout and recharge your creative batteries by spending time in nature. Being surrounded by earthly beauty helps you relax and come back into your body. Balance your seriousness and obsessive focus with fun activities, which might seem frivolous, but in fact reward you with increased inspiration.

Sex, death, mysteries, conspiracies, secrets and anything taboo or related to the Underworld are your creative domain. With your acute intuitive perceptions, you excel at research, investigation and excavation -- talents that could find expression through writing, journalism or documentary films. Music, acting and the visual arts provide outlets for your emotional intensity. Whatever form your creative expression takes, your higher creative mission is to reveal hidden truths and alert people to what is truly important.

Famous Scorpio Creators: ANTHONY KIEDIS, GEORGIA O'KEEFE, GRACE SLICK, JODIE FOSTER, JONI MITCHELL, KURT VONNEGUT, MARTIN SCORSESE, PABLO PICASSO, ROBERT MAPPLETHORPE, SYLVIA PLATH

Sun in Sagittarius
or in the 9th House

"Expansion, that is the idea the novelist must cling to,
not completion, not rounding off, but opening out."
- E. M. Forster

Your creative energy expands consciousness, inspires faith, and opens minds and hearts. Sagittarius is the outlaw and adventurer of the Zodiac, crossing borders and boundaries in search of the ultimate Truth. Diving into the mystery of the creative process, you deepen your faith and intuition.

Fascination and enthusiasm lure you in multiple directions, often all at the same time. Adventures to foreign countries and interactions with distant people, ideas and cultures fuel your creative fire. Your physical and philosophical journeys inspire feelings of freedom and possibility -- a highly creative state of being.

Righteousness and certainty, the Sagittarian shadow, drain your creative vitality. Your creative risk is to remain innocent and open, always an explorer, transforming and deepening your vision and beliefs. When you're willing to learn from anyone and anything, you step into your highest creative role -- teacher.

Cynicism -- a lack of faith in yourself and the universe -- is a sign that your inner artist-child needs some attention. Sagittarian expansiveness can lead to workaholism and other forms of over-extension, and you might neglect down time and play time. The child within needs to get out and burn off steam. Running, hiking, dancing, skiing and snowboarding might be especially appealing (Sagittarius rules the thighs). Time in the wilderness restores your sense of wonder, and heightens your intuition, a great creative resource.

You might synthesize your diverse talents and interests into a unique form of creative expression. You have a special affinity for storytelling, and could be drawn to writing, film or music. You have a natural affinity for comedy and love to lighten the mood and make people laugh. Whatever the form, your creative offering takes people to places they've never been, making the world a more expansive place.

Famous Sagittarius Creators: EMILY DICKINSON, JIMI HENDRIX, JON STEWART, MADELEINE L'ENGLE, SARAH SILVERMAN, SINEAD O'CONNOR, TINA TURNER, WALT DISNEY, WILLIAM BLAKE, WOODY ALLEN

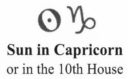

Sun in Capricorn
or in the 10th House

"Determination was never the question."
- JIM CARREY

Capricorn builds empires -- envisioning, establishing and organizing systems and structures, both tangible and intangible. Determined and persistent, the Mountain Goat climbs, step by cautious step, to the highest peak. Both visionary and pragmatic, you dream big and are willing to do the work to bring your vision into reality. You take your creativity seriously, applying high standards of quality, longevity and integrity to everything you offer to the world.

Ruled by Saturn, the wise old man in the solar system, you're likely to achieve the height of creative power in later years. You set ambitious goals, and then move slowly but persistently toward them. Self-discipline, patience and solitude are your creative resources.

Don't let perfectionism stifle your creativity. The fear of making a mistake can lead to procrastination and paralysis. Your creative risk is simply to start where you are, releasing attachment to the outcome, and the need for approval. Trust that, if you can imagine it, you can make it happen, and take one small step that affirms your faith.

You can recharge your creative batteries by tuning into your inner world of dreams and emotions. Extremely sensitive and naturally reserved, you may have a tendency to shut down, ignore or try to control intense feelings. Art offers a safe outlet for expressing the depth of your emotions, and the more you get in touch with your feelings, the easier it is to access the creative flow. Ask your dreams for creative solutions to challenges in your waking life, enlisting your unconscious in service to your worldly goals.

With your workaholic tendencies and uber-responsible nature, your inner child might feel more like a somber old man or woman. You may need to make a conscious effort to liven up the child within, by scheduling dates for fun into your planner. The more you connect with your playful side, the more your creativity flows. Aspire to emulate Pan, the mythological satyr (half-man, half-goat) playing his flute and kicking up his heels with the woodland nymphs. Spending time in nature, hiking and mountain climbing energize you.

As an Earth sign, you might be drawn to arts with practical applications -- carpentry and other forms of building, gardening, ceramics and crafts. You may build your empire through writing, film or visual arts, creating imaginary worlds that reflect your higher vision. Music (both playing and listening) helps you drop into your emotions and connect with your deepest passions.

Famous Capricorn Creators: ANNIE LENNOX, DAVID BOWIE, DENZEL WASHINGTON, DIANE KEATON, FAYE DUNAWAY, HENRI MATISSE, JANIS JOPLIN, JIM CARREY, JRR TOLKIEN, PATTI SMITH

☉ ♒

Sun in Aquarius
or in the 11th House

"Whatever our theme in writing, it is old and tired.
Whatever our place, it has been visited by
the stranger, it will never be new again.
It is only the vision that can be new;
but that is enough."

- EUDORA WELTY

Your innovative creative energy breaks down old structures and takes humanity into the future. Aquarius is the sign of the genius, inventor, revolutionary and humanitarian. Always at least one step ahead of society, you're likely to feel different from everyone else. When you accept and revel in your role as an outsider and rebel, you're able to tap into your highest creative potential.

As an Air sign, your primary creative tool is your highly-developed brain. Your creativity might find expression as an innovator in the realm of science, technology or politics. Or, you could apply your gifts of accurate observation, visionary perspective and wit as a writer, particularly in science fiction or other futuristic genres, or social or political commentary.

No matter what medium you're working in, what's important is that you follow your own path and share your unique vision. The ultimate creative risk you need to take is the risk of being yourself, exposing your eccentric, original and rebellious nature. Often this risk involves breaking with tradition and making a radical departure from your family of origin. By freeing yourself from personal and social conditioning, you tap into deeper levels of creativity, and can assist others to wake up to their inner truth.

While generally open-minded and forward-thinking, you may have a tendency to get attached to certain ideas or beliefs and become resistant to new perspectives. When intellectual stubbornness sets in, your creative energy diminishes. If you notice resistance, you can free up your creativity by getting curious and asking yourself: What am I protecting by resisting this new idea/belief/perspective? Letting go of old ways of thinking and opening to the new helps you stay in the creative flow.

Your creative fire burns brightest when you feel your work contributes to the greater social good or to a higher spiritual purpose. If you're feeling burnt-out, you can recharge your creative batteries by reconnecting with your vision and clarifying your personal goals.

Linking up with like-minded, forward-thinking friends, taking a class or workshop in a new and exciting topic, and participating in a community project or event are other strategies for getting your mojo back.

With the Aquarian inclination toward being overly serious, your inner child might feel more like a somber old man or woman. You may need to make a concerted effort to get out of your brain and play. Paying attention to the here-and-now joys of life, rather than always focusing on how things could be in your imagined ideal reality, enhances your creativity and your feeling of freedom.

Famous Aquarian Creators: ALICE WALKER, AMADEUS MOZART, BOB MARLEY, EDDIE IZZARD, ELLEN DEGENERES, JACKSON POLLOCK, OPRAH WINFREY, PAUL NEWMAN, VIRGINIA WOOLF, YOKO ONO

Sun in Pisces
or in the 12th House

*"Imagination is more important than knowledge.
Knowledge is limited. Imagination
encircles the world."*

- ALBERT EINSTEIN

Your creativity generates magic, healing, love and compassion. Pisces the Fish is the visionary, mystic and dreamer, journeying into the ocean of consciousness, and bringing to the surface what has been lost or submerged. You have a special affinity with music, film, dance and poetry. But, with your many talents, your creativity could take any number of forms.

As a Water sign, you perceive the world primarily through your highly sensitive emotions. You intuitively sense the interconnectedness of all things, understanding that, at the deepest level, we are all one. This awareness enables you to create beyond your own actual experience, as you feel your way into different characters and alternate realities. You can always trust your intuition to guide you in the right direction.

Without strong boundaries and conscious awareness, your sensitivity can become a creative liability. You might easily absorb the thoughts and emotions of people in your environment and beyond, resulting in confusion about your own vision and intuition. Feeling so much a part of everyone else, you might lack a strong sense of individuality, and fail to recognize your unique creative gifts.

Your creative risk is to take action toward manifesting your vision. You might need to set boundaries with people in your life in order to carve out time for creativity. Solitude is necessary for clarifying your dreams and goals, and for accessing the deepest levels of your imagination. Perhaps more than any other sign, you need a creative outlet to keep you sane, as creativity provides a healthy means of escaping the mundane.

Recharge your creative batteries with sleep, meditation and spending time in or near the water. An ocean is ideal, but baths also work. When you feel relaxed and blissed-out, you easily access the creative flow. Tendencies toward addictive or unconscious habits usually reflect a need for more retreat time. Remember you are of most service to others when you serve your own spirit.

Your inner child is a dreamer and yearns to get lost in fantasy worlds. Take her out to the movies, a magic show, or to beautiful places in nature to reawaken a sense of wonder. Connecting with the child within grants you access to your quirky sense of humor, which enhances your creativity.

Famous Pisces Creators: ANSEL ADAMS, AMY TAN, ANAIS NIN, DR. SEUSS, DREW BARRYMORE, ELIZABETH TAYLOR, JACK KEROUAC, MICHELANGELO, QUEEN LATIFAH, SPIKE LEE

Mars

Stoking the Creative Fire

*"I've been absolutely terrified every moment of
my life and I've never let it keep me from
doing a single thing I wanted to do."*
— GEORGIA O'KEEFFE

Mars is the planetary Warrior that represents power, passion, desire and will. When Mars is suppressed or ignored, you can experience the shadow side of this energy -- anger, frustration, fear and depression. Mars teaches you how to develop confidence, courage, strength and individuality by doing the things that challenge or even terrify you.

Mars's sign shows how to activate your creative passion, inspire motivation, and break through creative blocks. It also reveals what you may have to fight for, or against, in order to express yourself.

Mars in Aries
or in the 1st House

"Life shrinks or expands according to one's courage."
- ANAIS NIN

As the planetary ruler of Aries, Mars excels in the sign of the Ram, and your creative flame burns bright. Aries initiates the wheel of the Zodiac, and you long to go first, to lead, innovate and pioneer. In your creative life, this means taking the risk of improvising your own style and methods rather than following tradition.

The part of the body ruled by Aries is the head, and jumping headfirst into the unknown is your modus operandi. Trust your gut instincts to guide your creative direction, always following the threads that excite you and ignite your passion. Your choices may not make sense to others (or even to you), but you build confidence by acting on impulse and being open to wherever they take you.

Your challenge is to continually return to the mindset of the beginner, to release what no longer holds energy for you, and start from scratch. Aries thrives on novelty, and you feel inspired when you encounter new ideas, people and places. If you feel stuck in your creative process, try doing something completely different -- either a fresh approach to your art, or a new form of expression altogether. Once you've shaken up habitual patterns, you can return to your work with an innocent perspective and renewed enthusiasm.

Aries is the archetype of the Warrior, and you approach your creativity -- and the rest of life -- as if going into battle. You might work very intensely on creative projects in short bursts of energy, and then need periods of rest and rejuvenation. Boredom and depression can signal that your inner Warrior needs a new and exciting creative challenge. Take time to identify your deepest desire, then take one action step toward fulfilling your creative dreams.

Mars in Taurus
or in the 2nd House

"Sometimes you've got to let everything go -- purge yourself. If you are unhappy with anything... whatever is bringing you down, get rid of it. Because you'll find that when you're free, your true creativity, your true self comes out."

\- TINA TURNER

With Mars in earthy and pragmatic Taurus, you direct your creativity toward tangible results. Taurus the Bull is the

73

farmer and the builder, generating abundance, prosperity, stability and comfort. In its highest expression, Taurus is the Earth Steward, taking practical action to nurture and cultivate the planet.

Set realistic creative goals, and move toward them step by step. Once you get started -- which might take a little while -- you pursue your goal relentlessly. The Bull's persistence can be an immense creative asset, giving you the strength and stamina to see your vision through to the end. When what you're creating reflects your deeply-felt values, you easily access the creative flow.

A lack of inspiration usually signals that it's time for a change of direction. Your creative risk is to shake up the existing order by releasing what you've outgrown -- beliefs, old emotional attachments, behaviors, possessions or relationships. You might fear the insecurity that change provokes, but trust that, by acting on your true desires, you will ultimately feel more secure and comfortable.

Creative inspiration comes from the Earth, whether in the woods or your own back yard. Make time for experiencing stillness and silence, for appreciating natural beauty, and for noticing what you are grateful for right now.

♂ Ⅱ

Mars in Gemini
or in the 3rd House

"Close the door. Write with no one looking over your shoulder. Don't try to figure out what other

people want to hear from you; figure out what
you have to say. It's the one and only
thing you have to offer."

- BARBARA KINGSOLVER

With Mars in the multiply-talented sign of the Twins, your creativity could travel in many diverse directions. Gemini is ruled by fast-moving Mercury, the Messenger God, and you move speedily through life, following your insatiable curiosity as your guide.

You don't have to journey far to find inspiration. Your wide-open and inquisitive mind is easily fascinated by all varieties of people, places and circumstances. If you're feeling blocked or stuck in your creative process, you probably need to encounter something new. Reignite your inspiration by traveling to an unfamiliar location, reading a book or taking a class on a subject that intrigues you, or experimenting with a new form of creative expression.

Your creative energy might be drawn in multiple directions at once, but don't fritter away your fire over-analyzing every possible path. With such an active mind, and the ability to perceive multiple perspectives at once, there's a danger of endlessly spinning options through your mental gears and never taking action. Risk committing to a course of action, trusting that, no matter which path you take, you'll get where you need to go. Approach your creative expression -- and the rest of life -- as an experiment, curious to see how it all unfolds.

Mercurial by nature, you have the power to shape-shift, and this adaptability and flexibility serve your creative process by enabling you to go with the flow when circumstances change. However, beware of being too much of a chameleon, thereby losing sight of your own creative vision. Creativity is an inner process and requires separating yourself from external

75

input from time to time. You develop confidence and courage by clarifying your unique truth and sharing it with the world.

Mars in Cancer
or in the 4th House

"The great majority of artists are throwing themselves
in with life-preservers around their necks,
and more often than not it is the life-
preserver which sinks them."

\- HENRY MILLER

Cancer is ruled by the watery and ever-changing Moon, whose domain is the subconscious. With Mars in the sign of the Crab, your creative power is fueled by your feelings. The more you're willing to explore your emotional depths, the more inspired you'll feel.

You can activate your creative passion by first discovering what you feel strongly about. Acutely sensitive, you easily pick up on the thoughts and feelings of people around you, so you might need time alone in order to get clarity. Mine your dreams and imagination for clues to your creative direction, noting any recurring themes or synchronicities. Like the Crab, you might move sideways, but you have the tenacity and resourcefulness to follow through on your creative goals.

Don't let the fear of being seen keep you hidden in your shell. You build your confidence by taking the risk of coming out from time to time and sharing your many creative talents. When you start feeling drained and depleted, it's time to return inward to nurture yourself and replenish the creative well.

Feeling stuck or blocked in the creative process can signal the need to take a risk. In your quest for safety and security, you may have become attached to certain methods and approaches that no longer work. Or, the creative goal itself might have lost energy for you. Be willing to change in order to move toward what you genuinely desire in present time. Trust your feelings, dreams and intuition to always lead you in the right direction.

♂ ♌

Mars in Leo
or in the 5th House

"To be yourself in a world that is constantly trying to make you something else is the greatest accomplishment."

- RALPH WALDO EMERSON

Leo the Lion is the sign of royalty, and with Mars in Leo, you long to be seen and celebrated. A Fire sign ruled by the Sun, Leo loves to bask in the light. You bring more light, love and joy to the planet when you express yourself from the heart and share your many creative talents.

You might be afraid that if you shine too brightly and are too successful, people will be envious and won't love you anymore. On the other hand, you might worry that, if you express what's in your heart, you'll appear foolish.

Your challenge is to cultivate unconditional self-love, giving yourself the respect and adoration you desire from others. You build confidence by taking one small step each day toward reaching your creative dreams. Releasing attachment to what anyone thinks gives you the courage to take risks and approach your creative process as play. When you're following your heart, rather than others' opinions, your creativity reaches its highest expression.

Feeling blocked in your creative process could signal that you need to have more fun. Engaging in playful activities brings you into your heart and into the present moment. From this childlike state of innocence, you easily tap into the creative flow.

♂ ♍

Mars in Virgo
or in the 6th House

"Get it down. Take chances. It may be bad, but it's the only way you can do anything really good."
- WILLIAM FAULKNER

Virgo signifies the archetype of the Servant, and you feel passionately inspired when contributing your skills and talents toward the greater good. Virgo the Virgin excels at purifying, perfecting and healing, and as an Earth sign wants to create tangible results.

Your innate perfectionism is of great use in the final phases of the creative process. With your clear vision, accuracy and precision, you are adept at honing, editing and finalizing the details of any creative project. You hold high standards for your work, wanting to present only your very best efforts to the world.

Perfectionism becomes a liability if you are so afraid of making mistakes or falling short of your high ideals that you fail to act on your creative impulses. Your challenge is to simply accept yourself as you are, and risk jumping into the unknown. You perfect your skills and talents by being willing to make mistakes.

If you're feeling blocked, you might be trying too hard to control the creative process. Letting go, following your intuition, and releasing your attachment to the outcome reconnect you with the creative flow.

Your creative power lives in the present moment. If you're overly focused on your vision of how things could or should be, or if you're staring at the next task on your to-do list, you're living in the future. Get grounded in the present by taking a few minutes to stretch, go for a walk, breathe deeply, meditate, or dance to a song you love -- whatever brings you back into your body. Slowing down and taking the time to return to the present ultimately results in greater creative productivity.

Mars in Libra
or in the 7th House

"If we listened to our intellect, we'd never have a love affair. We'd never have a friendship. We'd never go into business, because we'd be too cynical. Well, that's nonsense. You've got to jump off cliffs all the time and build your wings on the way down."
- ANNIE DILLARD

With Mars in the sign of the Scales, you long to create balance, beauty, justice and harmony. Libra is ruled by Venus,

79

the Goddess of Love, and you feel passionately inspired when you're following your heart's desires.

Making decisions about your creative path -- and other aspects of your life -- might be challenging. With the ability to see diverse perspectives, your analytical mind can rationalize any course of action. Rather than getting stuck in endlessly weighing your options, tune into your feelings to identify what inspires excitement. Then, go for it -- take one action step to demonstrate commitment to your passion. Have faith that whatever creative path you follow will take you exactly where you need to go.

Maintaining creative inspiration requires a balancing act between solitude and socializing. You need time alone, engaged in your creativity, to cultivate inner peace and discover your deepest desires. When you're engrossed in making art, you quiet your busy mind and drop into your intuition, which provides valuable guidance for moving forward. You might need to set boundaries with loved ones in order to carve out this necessary time for yourself.

On the other hand (Libra's favorite expression), your creativity also requires the stimulation of connecting with a variety of people and perspectives, and being exposed to diverse forms of artistic expression. Visiting a museum, attending a concert, play or other cultural event, or going to a party can help fill the creative well and reignite your inspiration.

If you're feeling blocked in the creative process, discover where in your life you are out of balance and take the necessary steps to recalibrate.

♂ ♏

Mars in Scorpio
or in the 8th House

*"When I dare to be powerful -- to use my strength in
the service of my vision, then it becomes less
and less important whether I am afraid."*
- AUDRE LORDE

Mars in the sign of the Scorpion longs to explore the darkness and the depths of the Underworld. You feel passionately inspired by mysteries, secrets and anything taboo. Mars is the planetary ruler of Scorpio, and therefore excels in this sign, granting you tremendous strength, courage and perseverance.

Your creativity is not something you take lightly. You want your work to matter, to make a difference, and to communicate the truth. When you're emotionally invested in the creative process, your focus becomes extremely powerful. Your tendency toward obsession, potentially challenging in everyday life, can be a blessing in your creativity, fueling you with the stamina to see projects through to the end.

Trust your feelings to tell you when it's time to change direction in your creative path. Feeling stagnant or blocked is usually a sign to let go of the old and try something different. You might need a new mystery to solve, problem to dissect, or core truth to reach. To stay engaged in your creativity, you need to always follow your passions.

Balance your relentless intensity with periods of peace and relaxation in order to maintain your creative life long-term. Spending time in nature helps you decompress and reconnect with your deepest values.

♂ ♐

Mars in Sagittarius
or in the 9th House

"Life is either a daring adventure or it is nothing."
        - Helen Keller

The red planet can have a rocking good time in fiery and fun-loving Sagittarius, sign of the adventurer, gypsy and philosopher. You feel passionately creative when you're doing what you love and expressing your personal truth, and you have a talent for expanding people's vision, perspective and faith.

Sagittarius is symbolized by the Centaur -- a mythological creature with the lower body of a horse and the upper body of a man. To activate and maintain your creative passion you need to indulge both sides of your dualistic nature. The horse in you needs to get wild and run free, while the human half needs to investigate philosophy, religion and higher consciousness.

If your creative energy feels stuck, it's time to explore uncharted territory, either in the physical or intellectual realm. Traveling to new locales -- whether an exotic foreign country or an unfamiliar part of town -- stimulates your inner artist. Bring a journal and/or sketch book to jot down notes and impressions for future creative projects. Risky adventures -- like bungee-jumping, snow-boarding or mountain-climbing -- can also get your creative juices flowing.

Your "human" half feels energized by exposure to new ways of thinking, whether through reading about different religions, talking with people from foreign countries or with divergent perspectives, or taking a consciousness-raising or mind-expanding workshop.

You can become stuck when you think you've found The Truth, rather than experiencing your life as an endless quest. In all your creative pursuits, an innocent, childlike attitude and curiosity are your allies.

♂ ♑

Mars in Capricorn
or in the 10th House

"The question isn't who is going to let me;
it's who is going to stop me."

— AYN RAND

With Mars in Capricorn, you long for success and recognition, driven to reach the very top of whatever mountain you choose to climb. Both visionary and pragmatic, you dream big and have the practical skills to achieve your ambitious creative goals. According to traditional astrology, Mars reaches its highest expression in the sign of the Mountain Goat.

Capricorn is ruled by Saturn, Father Time, granting you the gift of timing, a great asset in your creative life. You instinctively know how much energy you need to put into any project, and are willing to take the time to ensure your work meets your high standards. Patience, perseverance, stamina and will power are your creative resources.

Capricorn rules the knees, representing the flexibility needed to move gracefully forward in your creative process. Although you would prefer to always be in control and have events unfold according to your precise plan, sometimes you have to go with the flow, acting on intuition and trusting in positive outcomes.

Feeling blocked or stuck in your creative process could signal that your inner world needs some attention. You may have become overly focused on external goals and lost touch with your vision and passion. Or, you may have set your goals so high that you're afraid to risk failure by taking action. Take time to commune with Mother Nature, listen to your dreams, and pay attention to your feelings. Solitude and reflection help you reconnect with the creative flow.

Mars in Aquarius
or in the 11th House

"When in doubt, make a fool of yourself. There is a microscopically thin line between being brilliantly creative and acting like the most gigantic idiot on Earth."
- PETER McWILLIAMS

With Mars in Aquarius, your creative passion is to awaken humanity through your innovative and revolutionary vision. Aquarius the Water Bearer brings enlightenment in the form of new ideas, fresh perspectives and inspired dreams for the future. When you contribute your creative energy toward manifesting your high ideals, you feel inspired and motivated.

You have a gift for creative collaboration with friends, groups and communities. Because you're ahead of your time, your ideas are likely to be different from everyone else's, and may even seem controversial. This is exactly as it should be, as your role is to shake up the status quo. You feel energized and enthusiastic when you take the risk of sharing your unique inner truth with others.

With high ideals for your creative expression, you might mentally map out how the process would unfold in your perfect world. Your challenge is not to get so caught up in thinking about the future that you neglect to take action in the present. At some point, you have to jump in and start where you are, risking the reality of imperfection. Be willing to adjust your plan once you get started, trusting your intuition to guide you in the right direction.

Feeling blocked or stuck in your creative process could signal that you're taking yourself or your art too seriously. Give your logical mind a break and do something playful and frivolous. Having fun takes you out of your brain and into your heart, and out of the future and into the present moment, reconnecting you with the creative flow.

Mars in Pisces
or in the 12th House

*"The most beautiful thing we can experience is
the mysterious. It is the source of all true art
and science. He to whom this emotion
is a stranger, who can no longer pause
and stand rapt in awe, is as good
as dead; his eyes are closed."*
- ALBERT EINSTEIN

Mars in the sign of the Fish longs to explore the ocean of consciousness, the imagination and dream world. Pisces is the dreamer, mystic and visionary of the Zodiac, intimately tuned into the realm of spirit. You feel passionately inspired when you're consciously engaging with your inner world and sharing your dreams and visions.

You tend to create in an organic, holistic way. With your gift of vision, you intuitively perceive the entirety of what you're trying to create, and have faith it will all work out in the end. You can trust your feelings, dreams and intuition to guide you in the right direction. The more you're willing to act on the deepest impulses from your inner world, the more confident and inspired you feel.

Identifying what exactly you want is the first and possibly most challenging step in the creative process. Mars can easily lose focus and direction in watery and diffuse Pisces, distracted by too many options, and overwhelmed by emotions absorbed from your surroundings. Wallowing in indecision dissolves your creative energy. Your challenge is to make a decision, any decision, and act on it. Once you choose your path, you easily access the creative flow.

Sensitive and compassionate, you may be afraid to take actions or express strong feelings that could potentially upset anyone. However, suppressing your emotions and desires blocks your creative energy, and can generate confusion and mistrust in your relationships. When you risk sharing your inner truth with others, you experience the genuine connection you seek, and can gain support for your creative goals.

Part II

Aligning with Natural Time

*"The energy-cycle of the year is not just a calendrical
affair: it is a cycle of growth and consolidation
fundamental to our very existence.... [I]t is
a cycle of subtle energy which is
very usable in our own lives, a
participation in the breathing
of Mother Earth."*
      - PALDEN JENKINS, *Living in Time*

The solar system is like a big clock, telling you what time it is. Astrology is a language for communicating with the planets, revealing the meaning and purpose of this moment in time. Is it time to push forward, or time to lay low and rest? Is it time to launch a bold new beginning, or to revisit the past and complete an old project?

Contrary to popular belief, astrology does not tell you whether this time is "good" or "bad." Instead, astrology simply describes the energies available in this moment, similar to a weather report. How you respond to and work with these energies determines the quality of your experience.

The underlying premise is that there's a purpose for each moment in time. When you're aware of that purpose and cooperating with the cosmos, you tap into the natural flow of time, and it's much easier to create effectively and successfully.

Our ancient -- and even more recent -- ancestors were well-versed in the practical art of astrology. The story of the sky was consulted to determine the optimum times for migrating, planting and harvesting crops, conceiving children, and initiating grand plans. Indigenous cultures, in which people live much closer to nature, continue to align with these cycles.

Although astrology is a complex science, there are simple and profoundly effective ways to work with planetary cycles that are accessible to anyone. Below are some suggestions for aligning with natural time to increase your ability to tap into the creative flow. Approach these suggestions with an attitude of experimentation and discover the results for yourself!

Solar Seasons

The Wheel of the Year

*"To everything there is a season, and a time
to every purpose under heaven."*
- Ecclesiastes 3:1

Seasonality is based on our Earthly experience of what appears to be the movement of the Sun -- the changing interplay of light and dark over the course of a year. The phenomenon of seasons is actually caused by the tilt of the Earth's axis, so that as the Earth orbits the Sun, different areas of the planet receive more or less light at different times of year.

Our bodies are naturally attuned to the seasons, longing to slow down and rest when the light is weak and the days are short, and to expand and create when the light is strong and the days are long. Honoring this natural rhythm supports the creative process -- as well as overall health and well-being.

In the wheel of the year, the Solstices and Equinoxes are traditionally considered major power times or "gates of power." Each Solstice and Equinox marks the beginning of a season, and initiates a new phase of the yearly cycle. The Solstices are the longest and shortest days of the year, while the Equinoxes are when the day and night are equal.

The following description of the yearly cycle is for the Northern Hemisphere. If you're in the Southern Hemisphere, simply reverse the Solstices and Equinoxes (i.e., exchange Winter Solstice for Summer Solstice, and Spring Equinox for Fall Equinox).

The Winter Solstice, which falls on or around December 21st, is the shortest day of the year, when the darkness reaches its height of power. The Sun, having traveled to its farthest point in the Southeast of the sky, appears to stand still (sol = Sun, stice = stands still) before changing directions and traveling North again. After Solstice, the light starts to grow and the darkness wanes.

Our ancient ancestors celebrated this holy day as the rebirth of the Sun God. Christmas is a more modern version of this ancient story, celebrating the rebirth of the Son of God. The Solstice is a deeply magical and mystical time of year, a time to reconnect with and strengthen your inner light, release the past, and plant a new vision for the coming year.

While the Winter Solstice roughly corresponds to our calendrical New Year (in the Northern Hemisphere), the Winter season is better suited to completions than new beginnings. The Sun is starting to gain in strength, but there isn't a lot of energy for launching a big new project. Instead, this is a time to finish up and reflect upon what you began at the previous Spring, and start to lay the groundwork and do the inner preparation for your next venture.

The more seasonally appropriate New Year begins at the Spring Equinox, around March 21st. Astronomically, this is when the Sun is directly over the Equator. The day and night are equal, and the light begins to ascend.

Traditional Spring Equinox festivals celebrated fertility, and this is a time when there's abundant creative energy available for new beginnings. The vestiges of this ancient holiday can be seen in the Christian Easter -- featuring eggs and rabbits, long-time fertility symbols -- and the Jewish Passover, which honors rebirth.

Astrologically (in the Northern Hemisphere), Spring Equinox is when the Sun moves into Aries, the first sign of the zodiac, initiating a new cycle. This is the best time to clarify your desires, set intentions, and plant seeds that will grow over the next year.

The Summer Solstice, around June 21st, is the longest day of the year, when the Sun reaches the height of its northern journey. Drenched in light, the Summer Solstice is traditionally a time to celebrate the bounty of nature and the joy of being alive.

The Summer season is a time for the fullness of self-expression and powerful creative output. Now it's time to manifest into physical form the seeds you planted at the Spring Equinox. At the end of Summer comes the harvest -- the results of your work and growth.

At the Fall Equinox -- around September 22nd -- it's time to evaluate what you've created, determine what is and isn't working, and restore harmony to any area that is out of balance. There may be something that needs to be released in order to come back into balance.

At Fall Equinox, the day and night are equal, and then the days grow shorter again, and darkness is on the rise. As the Winter approaches, there's an increasing awareness of the need to join together and share resources and energy. Having reached the peak of individual expression, it's time to turn attention to relationship.

The light wanes through the Fall season until the longest night at Winter Solstice, and then the cycle begins anew as the Sun God is reborn.

Lunar Cycles

Surfing the Tides

*"The lunation cycle is the prototype for the process
of progressive phases of the unfolding and continual
renewal of all of life forms. The moon's lunation
cycle carries the rhythmic beat of her dance with
the sun. It taps out the recurring pattern of
how life creates, fulfills, and destroys
itself, only to be reborn anew."*

— DEMETRA GEORGE, *Mysteries of the Dark Moon*

Just as the Moon influences the ocean's tides, the Moon's waxing and waning also reflect the rhythm of our own creative cycles. Synchronizing with the phases of the Moon is one of the easiest and most time-honored ways to "go with the flow" instead of "pushing the river."

The Moon completes one lunation cycle -- from New Moon to Full and back again -- over the course of about one month (29 1/2 days to be exact). Each cycle entails the birth, culmination and completion of a project, process or phase in our lives.

If you've got some astro-technical know-how, you could get more specific about what wants to be created by looking at the sign of the New Moon, and locating that New Moon in your personal birth chart. But just by simply following the phases of the Moon, you can greatly enhance your creative power.

Generally speaking, when the Moon is waxing -- when the lunar light is increasing -- you are opening to new possibilities and initiating new projects. This is an action-oriented time of pursuing goals and making things happen. After the Full Moon, as the light is decreasing, it's time to complete what you started and reflect upon what you've created.

New Moon Intentions

The lunar cycle begins with the New Moon or Dark of the Moon, a deeply mystical time when the energy is low and we naturally turn inward. Astrologically, the New Moon signifies the conjunction of the Sun and Moon as they occupy the same sign of the Zodiac. The Moon appears to be invisible because it's eclipsed by the rays of the Sun.

Reflect upon what you want to create for the coming month, clarify your intentions, and for added power, write down what

94

you want to manifest. The optimal time to set your intentions is the exact moment of the New Moon, or soon after. But the energy of the New Moon continues to be potent for about 24 hours, so don't worry if you have to wait and set your intentions a little later.

A simple New Moon ritual:

You'll need: a candle, paper and pen.

Light your candle and spend a few moments (or however long you need) just sitting, breathing, feeling into your heart, and getting grounded and centered.

When your mind feels clear and peaceful, pick up your pen and paper and write down your intentions -- what do you want to create? Astrologer Jan Spiller, author of *New Moon Astrology*, recommends writing down no more than ten New Moon wishes. (*New Moon Astrology* is an excellent resource for lunar magic.)

Over the years, I've experimented with different ways of writing my wishes. Usually I'll start with something like, "Dear New Moon, If it is in my highest good, and the highest good for all life everywhere, please grant me the following wishes..."

Sometimes I write my wishes in the form of "I wish..." or "I want to create..." and other times I write present-tense statements, as if my wish has already come true: "My writing flows through me effortlessly and joyfully" or "I achieve all my creative goals with grace and ease."

Once you've written your intentions, read them aloud slowly, feeling in your body what it would be like for each one to come true. You might want to try visualizing a scene of each intention manifesting in reality. Avoid including specific people in your intention-setting or visualizations, which would be a violation of magical etiquette. Instead of, "I want Brad to love me forever," you could wish, "I want to experience lasting love with the person who supports my highest good."

You can fold up the piece of paper and either stash it somewhere special (I have a box on my altar), or leave it out where you'll see it. When my list of intentions is in sight, I'm more likely to revisit it during the lunar cycle, which can be helpful in reminding me of what I want and keeping me on path. But it can also be nice to put them away, let go, and trust that they're already coming into being. I've had the experience of completely forgetting what I wrote, and then revisiting my intentions at the end of the lunar cycle and seeing that my wishes had come true!

Another option -- or additional intention-setting project -- is to make a New Moon collage, including images that represent what you want to create. This can be a fun activity to do with a friend or group.

Get Busy with the Waxing Moon

Start taking action on your New Moon intentions a day or two after the New Moon, around when the Moon reappears in the sky as a slender crescent. Taking action right on the New Moon is too soon -- there's not enough energy to work with yet. When the Moon is waxing, it's time to initiate new projects and open to new possibilities for existing projects.

About a week after the New Moon comes the First Quarter Moon or Waxing Half Moon, when, astrologically speaking, the Sun and Moon are forming a 90-degree angle or "square." At this point, you may encounter obstacles in moving forward with what you started. Reevaluate your course of action and determine the best approach for continuing on your path, or change course altogether.

Full Moon Clarity and Culmination

In the days approaching the Full Moon, you can feel the creative energy building -- now is the time to really go for it. The Full Moon occurs about a week after the First Quarter, but you can feel its influence for two days before and after the exact phase.

The high energy stimulates great productivity and there's a sense of things coming to culmination or fruition. Of course, as documented by police stations and emergency rooms, emotions are also running high -- hence the words "lunatic" and "lunacy."

With the Moon fully reflecting the Sun's light, you see the results of what you started on the New Moon. Astrologically, the Sun and Moon are now exactly opposite one another in the zodiac. Inspiration, revelations and breakthroughs are available during this lunar power time.

If you're trying to remove something (or someone) from your life -- old habits, weight, a relationship -- it's best to begin this process a day or two after the Full Moon.

Waning Moon Completions

After the Full Moon, it's time to complete what you started. As the light decreases you feel drawn to focus your energy, concentrating on the task at hand in order to follow through on commitments.

The Last Quarter Moon or Waning Half Moon comes about a week after the Full Moon. Once again, the Sun and Moon are at a 90-degree angle, and you could experience blocks or challenges to bringing your creation to completion. Refinement, paring down, and letting go are often necessary during this phase. Ideally, you also start to receive the fruits of your labor -- the end result of what you started about a month ago.

During the final days of the cycle, as the Moon's light fades back to darkness, it's time to go inward again and reflect upon your creations. "Being" rather than doing is appropriate during these dark nights, a time to rest and prepare for the next new beginning.

While every lunar cycle is different -- depending on the sign of the New and Full Moon and other planetary influences -- they all share a common pattern and rhythm. When you pay attention to and cooperate with the Moon's phases, you'll notice a big difference in how much more easily you're able to create what you want.

Mercury Retrograde

Slow Down, Back Up, Review and Re-do

*"If you're having difficulty coming up with new ideas,
then slow down. For me, slowing down has been a
tremendous source of creativity. It has allowed
me to open up -- to know that there's life
under the earth and that I have to let
it come through me in a new way."*

— NATALIE GOLDBERG

Although Mercury Retrograde gets a bad rap, as with every cosmic influence, there is a deeper meaning and purpose. When you know how to work with -- rather than resist -- the energy, Mercury Retrograde can be both productive and beneficial.

A planet is Retrograde when it appears to slow down, stand still in the sky, and then reverse directions. Of course a planet never actually goes backwards, but astrology is based on how the sky appears from our Earth-based perspective. Following the ancient law "as above, so below," when a planet turns Retrograde, we are also advised to slow down, back up, and turn our attention to the past.

Mercury goes Retrograde three or four times a year, for about three weeks at a time. However, the Retrograde influence extends for longer than those three weeks -- for a few weeks on either side of the actual Retrograde period. This means that, when you add it all up, we're under the Mercury Retro influence for nearly half of every year!

In astrology, Mercury rules the mind, communication, electronics and transportation. During Mercury Retrograde we don't get to operate in the ways that we're used to. Life slows down -- unacceptable in our fast-moving world -- and our rational minds become less reliable. Computers, cars and all electronic equipment are more likely to break down or malfunction. Miscommunications and misunderstandings add to the stress, frustration and fatigue that are common Mercury Retro symptoms.

So where's the silver lining here? While it's not the easiest or best time to move forward, Mercury Retro is the Universe's catch-up period -- a great time to complete or re-do old projects, and to reconnect with old friends and loved ones. It is also a time to rest, relax, retreat, and give your logical mind a break while tuning into your intuition -- which is more powerful at this time.

In terms of your creative process, consider that there's something from the past that needs to be taken care of before you can move forward. Resolving the past frees up energy for the future. You may also gain helpful intuitive insights and view an artistic project from a fresh perspective. If you're a writer, Mercury Retro is an ideal time for editing.

The sign (or signs) that Mercury is in while Retrograde will give more insight into the themes of each particular Retrograde period. With a copy of your birth chart and some astro-technical know-how, you can discover which house Mercury is traveling through to get clear on what wants to be revisited, reconsidered, re-done or completed in your own life.

Follow these guidelines for best results:

DO:

· slow down, rest, retreat, reflect, and seek higher and new perspectives

· reorganize, reread, rewrite -- basically, all the "re-" words

· back up your computer data!

· do your research and otherwise prepare for new projects

· resolve issues from the past and reconnect with old friends, etc.

- allow extra time to get to appointments and double-check details

- check in frequently with others to clarify communications

- keep your sense of humor, and practice patience!

DON'T

- initiate new projects

- make major purchases -- especially cars or electronics

- sign contracts or file law suits

- make long-term commitments

- start a new relationship or partnership

Conclusion

Building a Creative Life

"Every artist was first an amateur."
- RALPH WALDO EMERSON

The information in the previous chapters has offered insight into the needs, potential blocks, and innate gifts of your inner artist, and how to cooperate with planetary cycles for best results. Below are some suggestions for moving forward with building the creative life you desire.

Start small

*"Great things are not done by impulse, but by a
series of small things brought together."*
- VINCENT VAN GOGH

"I don't have time" and "I can't afford it" are favorite excuses of would-be artists. But you don't need hours of free time or huge amounts of money to express your creativity. Throughout history there are numerous examples of great artists who had less time and less money than you probably do, and nevertheless managed to make art.

The key is to start small, and start where you are. Even spending just 15 minutes a day on your art can make a tremendous difference in your life. Julia Cameron says, "Don't make time, steal it."

Find support

There's a popular perception that great artists are rugged individuals who make their creativity happen through sheer will alone. This may be true for some, but most creators have a team of support people who make it possible for them to do their work. I like to read the acknowledgements pages of books to remind me of this fact.

So please get the support you need. Make "artist dates" with friends, find or start a support group for like-minded artists, or take a workshop in your chosen field. You might consider working with a creativity coach, finding a mentor, or teaming up with an artist buddy to offer mutual encouragement and help hold each other accountable. When selecting someone to support you, be sure that person genuinely values your creativity and wants you to succeed.

Set goals and make realistic commitments

"I don't need time, I need a deadline."

\- DUKE ELLINGTON

Let yourself dream about your ideal creative life and write, paint or collage a detailed vision of what that looks like. Then, commit to a realistic plan to move toward your goals.

In my own experience, deadlines are essential for completing a creative project. Otherwise, my inner procrastinator-perfectionist takes over. So I let peer pressure and my people-pleasing tendencies work to my advantage by "hiring" a friend to hold the deadline for me and hold me accountable. For a big project, it can be helpful to set a series of smaller deadlines.

Study successful artists

"If people knew how hard I worked to get my mastery,
it wouldn't seem so wonderful at all."

- MICHELANGELO

It's easy to be dazzled by an artist's brilliance, and imagine they were just lucky enough to be born endowed with incredible talent that normal people like you and I will never possess.

But when you study the lives of famous artists, you discover they are, in fact, human -- they experience self-doubt, insecurity and fear, just like everyone else. Their main keys to success seem to be the willingness to take risks, the persistence and determination to keep going, and a strong belief in themselves and their creative vision.

Read biographies or watch documentaries and biopics about famous artists you admire to discover how they were able to succeed, and to inspire you to keep moving toward your creative dreams.

Here are some of my favorite movies about artists and their creative process:

BELIEVE: *The Eddie Izzard Story*
(a documentary about this British comedian)

105

BUKOWSKI: *Born Into This*
(a documentary about writer Charles Bukowski)

DAVID BOWIE: *Spiders from Mars: Interviews*
(a series of interviews spanning many years of Bowie's career)

FRIDA
(a biopic about artist Frida Kahlo)

INDEPENDENT LENS: *Trudell*
(a documentary about poet-activist John Trudell)

IT MIGHT GET LOUD
(a documentary about guitarists Jimmy Page, Jack White and The Edge)

JONI MITCHELL: *Woman of Heart and Mind*
(a documentary about this singer/painter)

METALLICA: *Some Kind of Monster*
(a documentary about the creative process of this metal band)

RIVERS AND TIDES: *Andy Goldsworthy Working with Time*
(a documentary about this artist who works with nature)

Honor your uniqueness

*"What is it you plan to do with your
one wild and precious life?"*
- MARY OLIVER

Most importantly, remember that you were born with a unique creative gift, yours to offer to the world, and only you can bring it forward. The world is waiting. What are you waiting for?

R E S O U R C E S

Helpful Books on Creativity

Julia Cameron, THE ARTIST'S WAY: *A Spiritual Path to Higher Creativity*, Jeremy P. Tarcher/Putnam, 2002.

Michele Cassou and Stewart Cubley, LIFE, PAINT AND PASSION: *Reclaiming the Magic of Spontaneous Expression*, Jeremy P. Tarcher/Putnam, 1995.

Natalie Goldberg, WRITING DOWN THE BONES: *Freeing the Writer Within*, Shambhala Publications, 1986.

Anne Lamott, BIRD BY BIRD: *Some Instructions on Writing and Life*, Anchor Books, 1995.

Sark, MAKE YOUR CREATIVE DREAMS REAL: *A Plan for Procrastinators, Perfectionists, Busy People and People Who Would Really Rather Sleep All Day*, Simon & Schuster, 2004.

Pat Schneider, WRITING ALONE AND WITH OTHERS, Oxford University Press, 2003.

Twyla Tharp, THE CREATIVE HABIT: *Learn It and Use It for Life*, Simon & Schuster, 2003.

Nina Wise, A Big, New, FREE, HAPPY, UNUSUAL LIFE: *Self-Expression and Spiritual Practice for Those Who Have Time for Neither*, Broadway Books, 2002.

R E S O U R C E S

Helpful Books on Astrology

Caroline Casey, **Making the Gods Work for You: The Astrological Language of the Psyche,** Three Rivers Press, 1998.

Liz Greene and Howard Sasportas, **The Luminaries: The Psychology of the Sun and Moon in the Horoscope**, S. Weiser, 1992.

Trish MacGregor, **Creative Stars: Using Astrology to Tap Your Muse**, St. Martin's Griffin, 2002.

Jan Spiller, **New Moon Astrology: Using New Moon Power Days to Change and Revitalize Your Life**, Bantam Books, 2001.

Jan Spiller and Karen McCoy, **Spiritual Astrology: Your Personal Path to Self-Fulfillment**, Simon & Schuster, 1988.

ABOUT THE AUTHOR

I've been in love with astrology for over 30 years – since reading Linda Goodman's Sun Signs at age 13. After studying on my own and secretly analyzing the charts of everyone I knew, I came out of the closet and started giving readings professionally in 1999. I'm now honored to pursue my passion for astrology full-time, as a reader, writer and teacher, and in combination with energy medicine. Above all, I work with astrology as a tool for healing, empowerment, personal growth and collective evolution.

I served as the in-house astrologer for Tarot.com in 2008, and as Chief Staff Astrologer for the website of Jan Spiller from 2009-2012. In 2011 I founded the Alcyone School for Engaged Astrology – an intensive apprenticeship program that prepares students to be professional astrologers.

Creative expression has been another strong thread throughout my life, although it wasn't until my Saturn Return (late twenties) that I started a committed exploration of this realm. Participating in a writing workshop based on the Amherst Writers & Artists method introduced me to a new approach to creativity that emphasized safety, support and authenticity, rather than struggle, isolation and competition. I was so taken with this method that I trained with Pat Schneider to become a writing workshop facilitator, and started leading workshops

– first in Brooklyn, New York, and then in Portland, Oregon, where I founded Portland Women Writers.

Over the past decade, I've also explored creativity through process painting, working with Stewart Cubley of The Painting Experience, and through ecstatic dance. These days I find myself drawn to making collages as a way to access the intuitive wisdom of my subconscious mind and to tap into the collective unconscious. Most collages I make are inspired by astrology – either as an intention-setting visual for the New Moon, or to uncover deeper understanding of a certain planetary configuration in the sky or in my own birth chart.

Before surrendering to my passion for astrology, I thought I wanted to be an academic, and graduated Summa Cum Laude with a B.A. in English from Brandeis University, and earned an M.A. in Women's Studies from Emory University. The New York Open Center and the Esalen Institute provided further (and ultimately more satisfying) "graduate studies" in the fields of spirituality, personal development, and the healing and creative arts.

You can find out more about my work at **virgomagic.com**.